That Hideous Strength: How the West was Lost

Expanded edition

What people are saying about this book...

A very brave, fine book written with keen insight. It explains how an older worldview that once shaped the West and in which many Judeo-Christian ideas were embedded has been superseded by one in which those ideas have been uprooted. The brave new world which is dawning is one in which people liberate themselves, dominate the meaning of reality, and subject God—if he is still there—to their own ends. In this context, the church is in a decidedly countercultural position. It is here, though, that it really finds its voice. Here it is able to speak into our fragile and corrupting world and speak of the goodness, greatness and grace of God.

David F. Wells, Distinguished Research Professor,
Gordon-Conwell Theological Seminary

Our culture has undergone a dramatic shift in recent generations, and Christians need to see it for what it is. If you suspect a sinister underlying agenda, Melvin Tinker agrees and wants to expose it for you. Informed, insightful, and yet easily accessible, this is an important and most helpful book that will sharpen your understanding of the world you live in. I hope it will receive wide attention!

Fred G. Zaspel, Pastor, Reformed Baptist Church, Franconia, PA, Adjunct Professor of Theology, The Southern Baptist Theological Seminary

There are very few books I buy multiple copies of—this is one of them. *That Hideous Strength* is an essential primer for any Christian in seeking to understand what is going on in society today. The first edition was outstanding but limited because of its size. This new expanded edition overcomes those limitations, without becoming unwieldy or too heavy. This book should be on every church bookstall, and every Christian's bookshelf. And now I have to go and buy more of the revised edition!

David Robertson, Director of Third Space, a project of the City Bible Forum in Australia, former minister of St Peters Free Church in Dundee, Scotland; theweeflea.com

That Hideous Strength: How the West was Lost

The Cancer of Cultural Marxism in the Church
and the World, and the Gospel of Change

(Expanded edition)

Melvin Tinker

EP BOOKS

(Evangelical Press) Unit C, Tomlinson Road, Leyland,
England, PR25 2DY

www.epbooks.org
epbooks@100fthose.com

The original shorter edition of *That Hideous Strength* originally published in 2018 and still available as ISBN 978-1-78397-240-1.

ISBN: 978-1-78397-294-4

British Library Cataloguing in Publication Data available

To Don and Joy Carson

With gratitude for modelling how to apply
the whole of Bible to the whole of life

Contents

Foreword

THE CHURCH IN EVERY AGE HAS FACED THE QUESTION OF how the content and expression of the gospel is to be related to the wider social, political, and cultural context of the time. Christianity is always to some extent expressed through the forms available and in relation to the concerns of the world in which the church finds herself. And that means that every generation has to think very carefully about what the gospel means and how the church is to apply the Bible's teaching. Foundational to that task are both a solid grasp of the church's historic testimony and mission, and a clear understanding of the contemporary world.

This is why Melvin Tinker's book is so important and so helpful. The twentieth century witnessed the rise of theories of culture which strike at the very foundation of the way the Christianity has understood the world, destabilizing any and all attempts to claim that truth is a stable category, and reducing all truth claims to bids for power. Victimhood is now a virtue which places the claimant beyond criticism. And the West is to be damned for its exploitation, manipulation, and oftentimes annihilation, of various examples of the Other, be they those of other races, classes, or sexual preferences.

Christians should have some sympathy for such approaches—we acknowledge, after all, that the world is fallen and that the abuse of power, and the presentation of falsehoods as verities, are indeed very real phenomena. It is also clear that the West has blood on its hands. The history of slavery is only the most obvious example. Yet the last few years have witnessed the absorption of these critical theories by the church herself in a way that can only be described with some obvious irony as rather uncritical. Many in the church now seem to think that the church herself is a—perhaps *the*—major culprit in the dominant narrative of exploitation and victimization. And that is leading to a revision, or perhaps better, repudiation of, the church's historic theology, mission, and gospel.

That, in short, is what is at stake here. It is not that Critical Theory has nothing to say of interest or importance. As noted above, it does take seriously aspects of this fallen world. The problem is that, in itself, it offers no positive ground upon which to build. And as such, it is ultimately no friend of the Christian gospel or the church. It is rather another example of thinking which seeks to immunize human beings from their accountability to their Creator. By silencing the church, it silences God.

This is the underlying point which Tinker makes so concisely and yet so compellingly in this volume. This book cuts through the opaque verbiage with which Critical Theorists appeal to the pseudo-intellectuals who lap up their meanderings and by which they protect themselves from proper scrutiny. It is therefore a clarion call to clear thinking of which all who read it should take heed. <u>Critical Theory is part of the spirit of the age</u>. Tinker is a prophetic voice in pointing out this obvious fact and in helping us to navigate accordingly.

Carl R Trueman
Grove City College
October 2019

Preface

CHRISTIAN LEADERS WHO HAVE SOUGHT TO FULFIL THEIR calling to 'keep watch over the flock which the Holy Spirit has appointed them as overseers' (Acts 20:28) have always been aware of the shaping influence of culture. This is seen in Augustine urging his congregation not to attend public spectacles, for the Roman theatre was so steeped in pagan religion that he believed it would have a damaging effect on believers, especially in the area of morality. Things are a little more subtle for Christians living in today's West, as evidenced by the 'Frontline' PBS video entitled *The Persuaders*.[1] This is not the lavish, jaunty 1970's television series recounting the adventures of two debonair international playboys, portrayed by Roger Moore and Tony Curtis; rather, it is a serious exposé of the way marketing gurus go about shaping our desires and tastes through the use of words and images.

It is both fascinating and disturbing to watch.

---

1 See Kevin J. Vanhoozer and Owen Strachan, *The Pastor as Public Theologian: Reclaiming a Lost Vision* (Grand Rapids: Baker, 2015), p. 116.

What is especially striking are the methods used to sell products which people didn't particularly want (I am reminded of the cynics' definition of advertising as 'the art of getting people to buy what they don't need by describing it in ways they know are not true'). There was no question of presenting reasoned arguments for a product (the last thing you want people to do is *think*); instead, the goal was to capture peoples' *imaginations* through the use of stories and images. Forget the old cliché developed by the US military during the Vietnam War of 'capturing hearts *and* minds', the target is the heart *alone* which lies at the root of our desires.

Stories and images are powerful means of getting people to see things in a certain way, as well as representing what is claimed to be 'real'. This is something Robert Joustra and Alissa Wilkinson helpfully explore in their book, *How to Survive the Apocalypse.*[2] By providing a detailed analysis of a dozen or so examples of recent TV series and films, the authors show that the West's view of the future is rather bleak. While earlier generations would craft stories which tended to be optimistic—seeing humankind on an upward climb towards a better and brighter future (think of Gene Rodenberry's *Star Trek*)—that view has now been exchanged for a more dystopian horizon. In the words of Woody Allen, 'The future isn't what it used to be'.

In her review of Joustra and Wilkinson's book, Rachel M. Billings usefully summarizes this idea:

---

2   Robert Joustra and Alissa Wilkinson, *How to Survive the Apocalypse: Zombies, Cylons, Faith, and Politics at the End of the World* (Grand Rapids: Wm. B. Eerdmans, 2016).

The crumbling 'worlds' these stories depict may be individual lives (as in *Breaking Bad*, *Mad Men*, and *House of Cards*) or global scenarios (as in *Her*, and *The Hunger Games*), projected earthly realities (*The Walking Dead*) or entirely imaginary realms (*Game of Thrones*).

And therefore, Billings goes on to suggest, these programmes reflect a completely human-centred way of thinking, and so not surprisingly the word 'self' frequently appears in Joustra and Wilkinson's critique of popular culture—in phrases such as 'self-authentication,' 'self-definition,' and 'self-fulfilment.' If everything is relative with no external values, and tradition is passé, what point of reference is there but the self? Billings continues:

Don Draper of *Mad Men* and Walter White of *Breaking Bad*, for example, both establish themselves as very successful men in some sense—one a heartless advertising executive and the other a ruthless drug lord. But because they have lost sight of any goal outside of their own cravings for power and its attendant privilege, their efforts at becoming 'themselves' end in self-destruction.[3]

There are two points to be made here.

The first is that stories and images are very powerful in portraying what we think the world is like or should be like, and today we are furnished with the means to do this both quickly and widely through modern technology. This

---

3 Rachel M. Billings, 'How to Survive the Apocalypse', http://www.reformation21.org/articles/how-to-survive-the-apocalypse.php [accessed: 18/12/2019]

is what sociologists refer to as 'connectivity'—we can more or less connect with anyone at anytime, anywhere about anything. More pertinent is the ability to have access to peoples' imaginations, and so their hearts, in a way which is unparalleled in human history.

The second is the representation of the 'self' as being the 'be all and end all' of human existence. Everything becomes self-referential. This raises the question: where has such a thoroughly 'egocentric' understanding come from which is being projected as 'reality'?

This book seeks to show how stories give insight into the state of affairs in the world and shape how we see the world, truly or falsely. It also unpacks the main ideology at work in the West (the main 'ism'); one which uses technology (especially the media and social networks) and education (or more accurately, propaganda), resulting in a thoroughly self-centred understanding of human beings and human existence.

We will look at two stories: one from the world of literature, the other from the world of the Scripture, which provide penetrating insights into the spiritual warfare which rages today in the West. The first story, *That Hideous Strength*, was written by C.S. Lewis over 70 years ago. The second story, to which Lewis's fictional work is linked, is the account of the building of the Tower of Babel in Genesis 11. Both will help us understand our times and assist us in formulating a Gospel response.

The ideology (or 'ism') we shall be exploring is cultural

Marxism. This is the machine which drives much of the Political Correctness which is stifling free thought and speech in our society today, as well as providing the philosophical matrix of much of the 'gender agenda'—homosexuality and transgender issues, and much more beside. I shall argue that this is a 'hideous strength', a particular manifestation of the 'principalities and powers' seeking to dethrone God and destroy man, and which the Tower of Babel episode is one of the earliest expressions of the corporate rebellion and arrogance which sets itself against the Creator and his creation.

In the course of this book I shall give some disturbing examples of the way a new totalitarianism is being introduced into Western society and the way the Church has colluded with this—at times actively, by buying into cultural Marxism (theological liberalism), or passively, by not concerning itself with such matters so long as one can be left to preach the Word (evangelical pietism). The picture which will be painted will be a bleak one, but, I trust, realistic.

However, the diabolical drama which is being played out in our schools, colleges, work places and government, needs to be placed within the bigger biblical drama of God's action in the world through his Son, the Lord Jesus Christ, and his people living as 'strangers and exiles'—called to stand against the world in order to win the world. The Christian who believes in the living God can never allow himself to become a cynic. Christians are not dewy-eyed optimists believing that peace of earth is just around the corner. Nor are they weary-eyed pessimists convinced that we are on an irreversible slide into the abyss. Rather, Christians are open-eyed realists who believe in a God who does not give up even when his people do.

The words of Rachel Billings in her review of *How to Survive the Apocalypse* is one with which I would agree,

> That's where the Gospel comes in, as I see it; it comes as a power from outside ourselves, interrupting human history and plans. As Christians, we point toward a hope that's far more radical than simply remaining hopeful and acting faithfully. We point toward a new world that God has promised, beyond the nightmares we've created, beyond the dystopias. We point toward our resurrection hope that if we accept Christ's vindication and transformation of us, we have no right to declare our own doom. Because our greatest hope in the midst of this failing world and its institutions is that nothing we can do will save it; only the action of God in Christ, intervening for a second time, can fully redeem and transform this broken creation. So, we wait in hope for a real Apocalypse—the culmination of the Gospel.

This present book is an expanded version of the previous edition. The original acted as a 'primer' and 'wakeup call' to enable Christians especially to try and understand what has been happening in our Western culture for the last few decades due to the influence of what is identified as 'cultural Marxism' or 'Critical Theory'. Many commented that it helped them make connections not seen before; for others, it was an 'aha moment', with the light suddenly being switched on as to why much of the Judeo-Christian foundations of the West have been eroded while the Church sleeps. A number of reviewers rightly said it would have been helpful to have had the works quoted referenced and expanded with footnotes. That failing has now been corrected.

As well as unpacking in more detail some of the ideas of cultural Marxists and the way their strategies are being worked out in our society, I have also sought to put more flesh on what the Church's response might look like by drawing attention to what has been called 'the Benedict Option' and developing the concept proposed by Charles Taylor—the 'social imaginary'. Another significant addition is an outline of the ideas of classical Marxism which places the current concern for cultural Marxism in its proper historical and philosophical context. It also serves to underscore that in many ways the 'new Marxism' is a revamping of the 'old Marxism' with consequences no less disastrous.

I would like to express my appreciation to Shirley Godbold for checking over the manuscript and the number of people who have sharpened my thinking on these issues, especially Tony Jones, Gavin Ashenden and Lisa Nolland. I am grateful to belong to a local church, St John, Newland, which seeks to embody the values and the vision of the Gospel—the 'biblical imaginary'—in all that it does. And last, but by no means least, I am as ever grateful for the constant support of my wife Heather and our family.

Melvin Tinker
St John Newland,
Hull
2020
Soli Deo Gloria

Chapter 1
A 2020 Space Trilogy

Introduction

C.S. Lewis was ahead of his time when he wrote the third of his Space Trilogy, *That Hideous Strength*, back in 1945.[1] John Mark Reynolds claims that it is 'the truest account of the state of the West written in the last one hundred years.'[2] Hyperbole perhaps, but one can't deny Lewis's remarkable prescience in being able to see what was coming down the cultural line. The title itself is taken from a sixteenth-century poem by Sir David Lyndsay called 'Ane Dialog' (1555), describing the biblical Tower of Babel as: 'The shadow of that hideous strength / Six miles and more it is of length.' In his preface, Lewis wrote: 'This is a "tall story" about devilry, though it has behind it a serious point which I have tried to make in my *Abolition of Man*.'

---

1   C.S. Lewis, *That Hideous Strength* (London: Harper Collins, 2005 [1945]).
2   Cited by David K. Naugle, 'The Devils in our World,' http://www.cslewis.com/the-devils-in-our-world/ [accessed: 18/12/2019]

In *The Abolition of Man* Lewis offered his thoughts on education, the tradition of natural law, and the necessity of moral oversight in the sciences to an audience at the University of Durham in February 1943. The 'serious point' referred to in the prologue of *That Hideous Strength* entertains the possibility that an intellectual elite of ideologues is capable of changing the way great swathes of a population considers what is 'obvious' and 'common sense', as well as being able to determine which views are permissible, which ideas are passé, and more than that, which beliefs are to be deemed 'dangerous'. Furthermore, there is the Promethean desire to use science and technology not so much to tame 'nature' but dominate it to the point of destruction or, as Lewis puts it in *The Abolition of Man*, 'The power of Man to make himself what he pleases means, as we have seen, the power of some men to make other men what they please.'[3]

What Lewis describes by way of fictional narrative is an outlook which derides all that is supernatural and reduces meaning to matter, or, to give it its proper title: naturalistic materialism. This is what Peter Berger describes as 'a world without windows'.[4] No longer do

---

3   C.S. Lewis, T*he Abolition of Man or Reflections on Education with Special Reference to the Teaching of English in the Upper Forms of School* (London: Oxford University Press, 1943), Ch. 3, para 5–10. For online version see www.samizdat.qc.ca/cosmos/philo/AbolitionofMan.pdf [accessed: 01/01/2020]

4   Peter L. Berger, 'For a World With Windows' in *Against the World for the World* ed. by P. Berger and R.J. Neuhaus (New York: Seabury Press, 1976), p. 10.

people see the world as a gift (a created order), but a given (a wholly natural order).[5]

This is one of the effects of the process of secularisation, which Lewis was certainly aware of, although he may not have used the term itself. Peter Berger defines this as, 'The process by which sectors of society and culture are removed from the domination of religious institutions and symbols.'[6] In other words, this is a movement of change which takes place through the *structures* of society, especially the spheres of science, technology, bureaucracy and the media which results in religious ideas becoming less meaningful and religious institutions more marginal. Of course, there is a subjective/intellectual side to secularisation—what is sometimes called the 'modern mentality' which was also in Lewis's sights. This has been described as, 'Man turning his attention away from worlds beyond and towards this world and this time (the *saeculum*).'[7]

---

5 See Kevin J. Vanhoozer, *Pictures at a Theological Exhibition: Scenes of the Church's Worship, Witness and Wisdom* (London: Inter Varsity Press, 2016), p. 36.

6 Peter L. Berger, *The Sacred Canopy: Elements of a Sociological Theory of Religion* (Garden City: Doubleday, 1967), p. 107. Similarly Bryan Wilson defines secularisation as 'the process whereby religious thinking, practice and institutions lose their social significance.' in Bryan Wilson, *Religion in Secular Society: A Sociological Comment* (London: C.A. Watts, 1966), p. xiv.

7 Harvey Cox, *The Secular City: Secularization and Urbanization in Theological Perspective* (London: SCM Press, 1965), p. 2. For a critical assessment of secularisation and a Christian response, see Melvin Tinker, 'Secularisation: Myth or Menace? An Assessment of Modern 'Worldliness', *Themelios*, 38:3 (2013), 402–16. It is important to distinguish between secularisation and secularism. Secularisation is a process whereas secularism is a philosophy and outlook.

One major consequence of secularisation, which Lewis resolutely opposed, is what Max Weber termed, disenchantment, (*Entzauberung*), where the 'magic' or 'mystery' of life is not just removed but unwanted and we simply apply reason and technology to life's problems with the consequence that matters of faith are deemed irrelevant.[8] This modernist outlook is summed up by the social scientist, Philip Rieff, 'What characterises modernity, I think, is just this idea that men need not submit to any power—higher or lower—other than their own.'[9]

When N.I.C.E. is nasty

The bulk of the plot of *That Hideous Strength* concerns the threat of the National Institute of Coordinated Experiments (forming the delicious acronym N.I.C.E.) with its aim to free humanity from nature. The symbol adopted by N.I.C.E., which is devoted to 'Technocratic and Objective Man,' is a muscular male nude grasping a thunderbolt.[10] The overall goal of the organisation is 'the scientific reconstruction of the human race in the direction of increased efficiency.'[11] The irony is that while the group eschews all that is supernatural—embracing a purely materialistic view of reality—Lewis portrays it as being under the direction of unseen, sinister spiritual

---

8   See Max Weber, *The Sociology of Religion* (1920).

9   See Os Guinness, *Dining with the Devil: The Mega Church Movement Flirts with Modernity* (Grand Rapids: Baker, 1993), p. 49.

10 Lewis, *That Hideous Strength*, p. 355.

11 Lewis, *That Hideous Strength*, p. 354.

forces, what he called '[dark] eldilic energy and [dark] eldilic knowledge'.[12] Lewis uses the term 'macrobes' for the demonic powers hovering from above, 'The structure of the macrobe, so far as we know it, is of extreme simplicity. When I say that it is above the animal level, I mean that it is more permanent, disposes more energy, and has greater intelligence.'[13] These are the 'rulers', 'authorities' and 'spiritual forces of evil in the heavenly realms' of which the apostle Paul speaks in Ephesians 6:12.

The main image of evil in the story is Alcasan's Head, the forerunner of 'a new species—the Chosen Heads who never die', separated from its body and kept alive artificially. In his helpful critique of the story, Pete Lowman suggests the various meanings associated with this figure.[14]

Firstly, according to Lowman, it stands for the 'rational processes operating in supposedly 'objective' separation from the moral law'. As Lewis says in the 1955 Preface, he is making the same point here as he did in his essay *The Abolition of Man*; and in the latter book he describes thinkers who are embracing this idea as 'men without chests [...] The head rules the belly through the chest—

---

12 Lewis, *That Hideous Strength*, p. 201. Lewis makes the same point in *The Screwtape Letters*, such that the demon's goal is to produce 'our perfect work, the Materialist Magician' who will use and even worship 'Forces' while denying the existence of 'spirits', (London: Fount, 1977), p. 39.

13 Lewis, *That Hideous Strength*, p. 352.

14 Peter Lowman, 'Chronicles of Heaven Unshackled', https://www.bethinking.org/ your-studies/chronicles-of-heaven-unshackled/5-that-hideous-strength [accessed 17/12/2019]

the seat [...] of emotions organized by trained habit into stable sentiments.'[15]

<u>Secondly, Lewis is using the amputated Head to stand for 'a rationalism that cuts itself adrift from or is hostile to 'Nature".</u> A third variant appears when N.I.C.E. initiate, Frost, compares humanity to an animal no longer needing a large body for nutrition and locomotive organs: 'The masses are therefore to disappear. The body is to become all head. The human race is to become all Technocracy'—and so sixteen major wars are scheduled for the twentieth century.'[16]

Lewis is not at all unabashed in bringing the supernatural to the fore at various points throughout the story, but in doing this he drew his strongest criticism. In one early review, George Orwell wrote, 'One could recommend this book unreservedly if Mr. Lewis had succeeded in keeping it all on a single level. Unfortunately, the supernatural keeps breaking in, and it does so in rather confusing, undisciplined ways.'[17] More recently, Rowan Williams has written of the destruction of the evil characters at the end of the story in the following way:

> 'Over the top', I think, is the only expression one can use for this. I think it's when the elephant breaks loose and comes into the dining room and begins trampling

---

15 Lewis, *The Abolition of Man*, p. 11.

16 Lowman, 'Chronicles of Heaven Unshackled'.

17 George Orwell, 'The Scientists Take Over: Review of *That Hideous Strength*,' *Manchester Evening News* (16 August, 1945), http://www.lewisiana.nl/orwell [accessed: 20/12/2019]

people to death that I feel something has snapped in the authorial psyche.[18]

However, this approach was quite intentional by Lewis, as he made clear in a letter to Dorothy L. Sayers written after receiving several negative reviews: 'Apparently reviewers will not tolerate a mixture of the realistic and the supernatural. Which is a pity, because (a) it's just the mixture I like, and (b) we have to put up with it in real life.'[19]

If it is the case that we are involved in a spiritual battle, as the Bible makes clear, Christians can't yield the field to the secularists, in fact, they have all the more vigorously to assert the supernatural for, as we shall see in due course, whatever the particular ideologies the church has to contend with, they are manifestations of forces which mere human means are unable to overcome. As Paul makes clear in 2 Corinthians 10:3–5:

> For though we live in the world, we do not wage war as the world does. The weapons we fight with are not weapons of the world. On the contrary they have divine power to demolish strongholds. We demolish arguments and every pretension that sets itself up against the knowledge of God.

Lewis was simply following the apostle Paul at this point.

---

18 Rowan Williams, 'That Hideous Strength: A Reassessment,' in *C.S. Lewis and His Circle: Essays and Memoirs from the Oxford C.S. Lewis Society*, ed. by Roger White, Judith Wolfe, and Brendan N. Wolfe (Oxford: Oxford University Press, 2015), p. 99.

19 Quoted in *C.S. Lewis: A Companion & Guide*, ed. by Walter Hooper (San Francisco: Harper, 1996), p. 231).

Science vs Scientism

The way in which the members of N.I.C.E. seek to realise the organisation's aims is <u>primarily through education but they also employ technology</u>. Lewis was aware that <u>ideas never remain hermetically sealed within the academy, they eventually flow out to shape society and more importantly influence *individual* human beings for good or ill</u>. Such individuals are represented in the story by the newly married Studdocks. In an edition of *Punch* published in August 1945, H.P. Edens wrote, 'It is Mr Lewis's triumph to have shown, with shattering credibility, how the pitiful little souls of Jane and Mark Studdock become the apocalyptic battlefield of Heaven.'[20]

Lewis's critique was not universally well received at the time. Some, like the humanistic scientist, J.B.S. Haldane, were particularly offended. Replying to Haldane's concerns, <u>Lewis said that scientists *per se* were not his target, but rather certain *trends* which were beginning to creep into society such as 'officials' using the power of a small group to subvert (the 'inner ring'), the exaltation of the collective with little concern for the individual, the 'Party' that obeys an impersonal force and believes in human progress using whatever means necessary to bring about the 'liberation' of people, especially those who do not yet realise they need liberating; and the way education</u>

---

20 Quoted in Gavin Ortlund, 'Conversion in C.S. Lewis's *That Hideous Strength*', *Themelios*, 41:1 (2016), 8–19 (p. 9).

in particular was being invaded by naturalistic and anti-religious indoctrination.[21]

This may well be, but there is little doubt that it was *scientism* as specifically represented by the likes of Haldane that Lewis had in his sights which means Haldane had every reason to take it personally.[22] Haldane was a leading proponent of what became known as 'social Darwinism' as seen in his essay, 'Eugenics and Social Reform.'[23] He proposed the optimisation of the human gene pool by preventing certain types of people from breeding. This was also championed by none other than Bertrand Russell who, in 1929, advocated the compulsory sterilisation of the mentally subnormal.[24] Russell argued that the state should have the power to forcibly sterilise all those regarded as 'mentally deficient' by appropriate experts and, he argued, the resulting reduction of 'idiots, imbeciles and feeble minded' people would be of such a benefit to society that it would outweigh any dangers of misuse.[25] Lewis saw the need to challenge such views, hence he wrote *That Hideous Strength*.

---

21 For Lewis's reply see C.S. Lewis, *Of Other Worlds*, (Harvest Books, 2002), p. 74. Also see Martha C. Sammons, *A Far Off Country: A Guide to C.S. Lewis' Fantasy Fiction* (Lanham: University Press of America, 2000), pp. 105–106.

22 Scientism is a wholesale philosophical movement which, as a matter of principle (not evidence), has no room for God or the transcendent. It is the attempt by some in the scientific community to piggy back on the prestige of science to popularise naturalistic materialism and is not very scientific at all. See Michael Stenmark, *Scientism: Science, Ethics and Religion* (Burlington, VT: Ashgate, 2001).

23 J.B.S. Haldane, *Possible Worlds* (New Brunswick: Transaction Publishers, 2001).

24 Bertrand Russell, *Marriage and Morals*, (London: Routledge, 2009).

25 See Alister McGrath, *C.S. Lewis A Life: Eccentric Genius, Reluctant Prophet* (London: Hodder and Stoughton, 2013), pp. 235–236.

Nothing Buttery

Lewis was accurate in describing the *Zeitgeist* which was to move so powerfully throughout the post-war West. I studied biological sciences at university in the 1970s and without a doubt the naturalistic materialism of the likes of Jacques Monod, Francis Crick and B.F. Skinner, with their reductionistic understanding of humans as being 'nothing but a bundle of neurological reflexes', was all the rage. The philosophical label which was attached to this approach was 'ontological reductionism'.[26] As early as the 1950s Professor D.M. MacKay dubbed this standpoint 'nothing buttery', which he showed to be philosophically bankrupt.[27] The offence this position is to plain common sense is ably illustrated by the story of B.F. Skinner's visit to Keele University to give a lecture. After Skinner had delivered the formal lecture, in which he emphasised an objective, mechanistic description as a *total* explanation of man's behaviour, he was invited to have an informal discussion with Professor MacKay who had chaired the meeting. Skinner was asked whether in fact he was interested at all in who he, the chairman, and others were. Skinner simply replied, 'I am interested in the noises coming from your mouth'![28] Such reductionism, however,

---

26 An expression of this in Lewis's novel is the comment by Frost that, 'Friendship is a chemical phenomenon; so is hatred.' *That Hideous Strength*, p. 353.

27 See D.M. MacKay, 'Man as a Mechanism' in, *The Open Mind: A Scientist in God's World*, ed. by Melvin Tinker (London: Inter Varsity Press, 1988), pp. 45–53.

28 In recent years there has been an interesting swing in the opposite direction, considering things holistically rather than reductionistically, so comments physicist Professor Paul Davies, 'As far as physics is concerned, mechanistic materialism has been dead for fifty years. It is rather curious that in molecular biology this

is still doing the rounds as we see from this bold assertion by Richard Dawkins:

> We are machines built by DNA whose purpose is to make more copies of the same DNA [...] Flowers are for the same thing as everything else in the living kingdoms, for spreading 'copy me' programmes about, written in DNA language. That is EXACTLY what we are for. We are machines for propagating DNA, and the propagation of DNA is a self-sustaining process. It is every living object's sole reason for living.[29]

More recently Kevin Vanhoozer has argued, 'I believe that in the years ahead the real flash point between science and theology will concern not the origins of the cosmos or even biological life on earth, but rather the nature of humanity. The real danger in the years ahead is a reductionism in our theories about what it is to be human.'[30]

This too is what Lewis saw to be the main issue at stake and in so doing proved that he was very much ahead of his time.

---

old-fashioned reductionism and mechanism still thrives, on the physics of the nineteenth century', in Keith Ward, *The Turn of the Tide*, (London: BBC publications, 1986), p. 46.

29 Richard Dawkins, 'The Ultra Violet Garden', *Royal Institute Christmas Lecture No. 4*, 1991.

30 Kevin J. Vanhoozer, 'From Physics to Metaphysics: Imagining the World that Scripture Imagines—An after dinner talk to the Henry Fellows and Stott Award Winners' (January 18th 2018)—unpublished.

Babies and Bathwaters

However, it is perhaps worth pointing out that in his zeal to alert the unsuspecting world to such dangers of natural materialism, Lewis may have overstepped the mark and so weakened his apologetic—throwing out the proverbial baby with the proverbial bathwater.

In *The Abolition of Man* Lewis mounts a protest against 'Baconian technology', claiming that both magic and applied science share a common ground in that they both try to subdue reality to the wishes of man. He condemned human dominion over nature as being hubris and praised the ancient wisdom of conforming to nature.[31] But this is more of a Stoic understanding, not a biblical one. For whatever reason, Lewis did not adduce biblical support for his position. A more measured and biblical perspective is offered by Professor Reijer Hooykaas:

> It is true that the results of our dominion over nature have been unhealthy in many cases; the powerful river of modern science and technology has often caused disastrous inundations. But by comparison the contemplative, almost mediaeval vision that is offered as an alternative would be a stagnant pool.[32]

However, Lewis's antipathy towards modern technology and perhaps a less than biblical understanding of nature,

---

31 *The Abolition of Man*, chapter 3.

32 R.J. Hooykaas, *Religion and the Rise of Modern Science* (Grand Rapids: Eerdmans, 1974), p. 74. See also, Melvin Tinker, 'Are Science and Christianity enemies or friends?' in *Touchy Topics* (Welwyn Garden city: Evangelical Press, 2016), pp. 158–163.

does not detract from some of his main points which have tremendous significance for us today, namely, the desire of humans to define reality (for example what it means to be human), the use of technology and education (propaganda) to achieve a re-visioning of the way things are, the power of a few ideologues using modern means to influence the many and the underlying spiritual battle which belies these things.

'The times they are a changin'

We have purposely spent some time looking at how Lewis foresaw the menace that results from a purely materialistic understanding of humanity. This not only helps us understand more fully the purpose and plot of Lewis's book, but gives a concrete example of what happens when humans surrender to another power other than God. But that was then, and this is now. In the relatively short span of 50 years the intellectual and cultural landscape of the West has morphed into something the scientists of Lewis's day, and those who have followed in their wake, could hardly have imagined; although in some ways they did prepare the way, not least by making Christianity appear to be an unviable intellectual option in the late-twentieth century.

The 'hideous strength' which Lewis described so imaginatively, and which the Tower of Babel episode embodies so eloquently, is very much at work today and needs to be confronted by the Church with every fibre of its being. Whilst not closing our eyes to the vestiges and dangers of scientism which still lingers, at least in the popular consciousness, there is a new manifestation of that 'hideous strength every much as powerful and dangerous as that which Lewis described, exhibiting the same characteristics and aims. The recent reminder by Kevin J. Vanhoozer is timely, 'For we wrestle not against flesh and blood, matters in motion, but against *isms*, against the powers that seek to name, and control, reality.'[33]

'Seeing as'—The Social Imaginary

We have already mentioned that *That Hideous Strength* is a significant product of Lewis's fertile imagination. But Lewis was aware that we all 'imagine' the world to be a certain way, including scientists. For the members of N.I.C.E. and those they represent in real life, the world is cold, cruel and callous. If those beliefs are followed through it will result in a dystopian world, not a utopian one, although such proponents would beg to differ. In H.G. Wells' *The New Republic*, the reader is shown what will happen to those so-called 'inferior races' in the new, Darwinian utopia:

> Well, the world is the world, and not a charitable institution, and I take it they will have to go [...] And the ethical system of these men of the New Republic, the ethical system which will dominate the world state, will be shaped primarily to favour the procreation of what is fine and efficient and beautiful in humanity— beautiful and strong bodies, clear and powerful minds

33 Vanhoozer, *From Physics to Metaphysics*.

> [...] And the method that nature has followed hitherto
> in shaping the world, whereby weakness was prevented
> from propagating weakness [...] is death [...] The men
> of the New Republic [...] will have an ideal that will
> make killing worthwhile.[34]

Exchange 'Men of the New Republic' for the members
of N.I.C.E. and you soon realise that Lewis's characters
were not purely fictional. What it came down to for
Lewis was: How do we view the world rightly? Which
'imagination' has the 'best fit' with reality?

For Lewis it was a matter of retrieving a former vision
of the world based on 'the doctrine of objective value, the
belief that certain attitudes are really true, and other really
false, to the kind of thing the universe is and the kind of
things they are.'[35]

More recently, the philosopher Charles Taylor has
explored the way in which we perceive life and so act
accordingly. He speaks of the 'social imaginary'—'a picture
that frames everyday beliefs and practices, in particular the
'ways people imagine their social existence.'[36] Vanhoozer
describes the idea as that

> Nest of background assumptions, often implicit, that
> lead people to feel things as right or wrong, correct or
> incorrect. It is another name for the root metaphor

---

34 Cited by Os Guinness in *Unspeakable: Facing Up To Evil in an Age of Genocide and Terror* (San Francisco: Harper Collins, 2005), p. 131.

35 Lewis, *The Abolition of Man*, p. 18.

36 Charles Taylor, *A Secular Age* (Cambridge, MA: Belknap Press of Harvard University Press, 2007), p. 171.

(or root narrative) that shapes a person's perception of the world, undergirds one's worldview, and funds one's plausibility structure.

He goes on to write,

A social imaginary is not a theory—the creation of intellectuals—but a storied way of thinking. It is the taken-for-granted story of the world assumed and passed on by a society's characteristic language, pictures, and practices. A social imaginary is not taught in universities but by cultures, insofar as it is "carried in images, stories and legends."[37] People become secular not by taking classes in Secularity 101 but simply by participating in a society that no longer refers to God the way it used to. "God" makes only rare appearances in contemporary literature, art, and television […] Social imaginaries […] are the metaphors and stories by which we live, the images and narratives that indirectly indoctrinate us.[38]

This, as we shall see, is a very useful tool to help us not only assess negatively what is happening in our present culture by the story of cultural Marxism, but more positively to present the Christian alternative arising out of Scripture.

---

37 Taylor, *A Secular Age*, p. 172.

38 Kevin J. Vanhoozer, *Hearers and Doers: A Pastors Guide to Making Disciples Through Scripture and Doctrine* (Bellingham: Lexham Press, 2019), pp. 8–9.

Man-made Religion

Lewis's reference to the Tower of Babel is pregnant with significance.

In the epigraph of *That Hideous Strength*, Lewis makes it clear that he sees the aims of N.I.C.E. as a comparable instance of human power extending beyond 'that limitation [...] which mercy had imposed [...] as a protection.' As we shall see, the Tower of Babel was not simply a *human* project; it was fundamentally a *religious* enterprise. It has long been recognised that Marxism is in effect a corruption of the Christian faith—having its own prophet (Karl Marx), Bible (*Das Kapital*), gospel (dialectical materialism), apostles (Lenin, Trotsky) and eschatology (the overthrow of capitalism and the establishment of the workers' ideal).[39] Similarly in Lewis's novel, while the 'progressives' disavow traditional Christianity, the language used and the zeal displayed to bring about a new world order are decidedly religious in nature. This is why Lewis has one of the main characters,

---

39 Marxism, according to Alasdair MacIntyre, is a 'secularism formed by the gospel which is committed to the problem of power and justice and therefore to the themes of redemption and renewal.' Alasdair MacIntyre, *Marxism: An Interpretation* (London: SCM, 1953), p. 18. One of the chief architects of neo-Marxism, Antonio Gramsci, is candid about the religious nature of socialism which must replace Christianity for the revolution to be successful: 'Socialism is precisely the religion that must overwhelm Christianity. [...] In the new order, Socialism will triumph by first capturing the culture via infiltration of schools, universities, churches and the media by transforming the consciousness of society.' Cited by Robert J. Smith, 'Cultural Marxism: Imaginary Conspiracy or Revolutionary Reality?', *Themelios* 44.3 (2019), p. 444.

the Reverend Straik, presenting the new science in religious terms:

> The Kingdom of God is to be realised here—in this world. And it will be. At the name of Jesus every knee shall bow. In that name I dissociate myself completely from all the organised religion that has yet been seen in the world [...] Therefore, where we see power, we see the sign of His coming, and that is why I find myself joining with communists and materialists and anyone else who is ready to expedite the coming. The feeblest of these people here has the tragic sense of life, the ruthlessness, the total commitment, the readiness to sacrifice all merely human values, which I could not find amid all the nauseating cant of the organised religions.[40]

The 'hideous strength' which is exerting itself in Western Society and the Western church today exhibits all the characteristics that the members of N.I.C.E. just described, and it is also comparable to the Tower of Babel. To this end, I want to use the story recorded in Genesis 11 as a parabolic lens through which we can view and come to understand what has been happening in our society and how it may be countered by the Gospel of Jesus Christ.

First, we must polish up the lens and return to Babel.

---

40 Lewis, *That Hideous Strength*, pp. 96–97.

Chapter 2
The Rabble at Babel

A PHRASE COINED BY C.S. LEWIS AND HIS FRIEND OWEN Barfield which has become well known is 'chronological snobbery'.[1] This refers to the widely held view that whatever belonged to an earlier time is inferior to the present simply by virtue of its temporal location. J.I. Packer summed this modern heretical position as 'the

---

[1] In his autobiography, Lewis describes how becoming aware of this fallacy began to undermine his own beliefs and draw him closer to the Christian faith, 'Barfield never made me an Anthroposophist, but his counterattacks destroyed forever two elements in my own thought. In the first place he made short work of what I have called my "chronological snobbery," the uncritical acceptance of the intellectual climate common to our own age and the assumption that whatever has gone out of date is on that account discredited. You must find why it went out of date. Was it ever refuted (and if so by whom, where, and how conclusively) or did it merely die away as fashions do? If the latter, this tells us nothing about its truth or falsehood. From seeing this, one passes to the realization that our own age is also "a period," and certainly has, like all periods, its own characteristic illusions. They are likeliest to lurk in those widespread assumptions which are so ingrained in the age that no one dares to attack or feels it necessary to defend them.' See C.S. Lewis, *Surprised by Joy* (London: Fount, 1982 [1955]), p. 167.

newer is the truer, only what is recent is decent, every shift of ground is a step forward, and every latest word must be hailed as the last word on its subject.'[2] However, as Lewis maintained, there is often great value in looking at something from a different age as it may offer a corrective to our own prejudices and limited perspectives. When we come to the account in Genesis 11 of the building of the Tower of Babel, early church commentators had some interesting insights.

In his discussion of the biblical narrative, James Austin provides this helpful summary:

> 'The men who migrate from the east in order to found Babylon are led by ambition and pride' (Chrysostom). 'Babylon is founded by Nimrod, as the capital of his kingdom. The inhabitants of Babylon construct the tower because in their pride they want to defy the power of God' (Augustine). 'The inhabitants of Babylon are giants who built the tower for their own salvation' (Pseudo-Dionysius). 'When God says, "Come, let us go down and there confuse their language," he is addressing the other persons of the Trinity' (Augustine). 'The Son is the one who is sent to the earth in order to confuse the language' (Novatian). 'Since the inhabitants of Babylon use the privilege of having a single language for evil purposes, God confuses their speech so that

---

2   J.I. Packer, 'Is Systematic Theology a Mirage? An Introductory Discussion,' in *Doing Theology in Today's World: Essays in Honor of Kenneth S. Kantzer*, ed. by John D. Woodbridge and Thomas Edward McComiskey (Grand Rapids: Zondervan, 1991), p. 21.

they are not able to understand each other anymore'
(Chrysostom). 'God sees that they are able to build the
tower because they speak the same language. Therefore,
he confuses their language in order to prevent them
from finishing their building' (Commodian).[3]

While this summary provides a mix of astute observation
and fanciful speculation, the main theological points are
sound and grounded in the biblical text of Genesis 11:1–9:

Now the whole earth had one language and the same
words. And as people migrated from the east, they
found a plain in the land of Shinar and settled there.
And they said to one another, "Come, let us make
bricks, and burn them thoroughly." And they had
brick for stone, and bitumen for mortar. Then they
said, "Come, let us build ourselves a city and a tower
with its top in the heavens, and let us make a name for
ourselves, lest we be dispersed over the face of the whole
earth." And the Lord came down to see the city and
the tower, which the children of man had built. And
the Lord said, "Behold, they are one people, and they
have all one language, and this is only the beginning
of what they will do. And nothing that they propose
to do will now be impossible for them. Come, let us
go down and there confuse their language, so that they
may not understand one another's speech." So the Lord
dispersed them from there over the face of all the earth,
and they left off building the city. Therefore its name

---

3 See James Austin, *The Tower of Babel in Genesis: How the Tower of Babel Narrative Influences the Theology of Genesis and the Bible,* (Grand Rapids: WestBowPress, 2012).

was called Babel, because there the Lord confused the language of all the earth. And from there the Lord dispersed them over the face of all the earth. (ESV)

United We Stand

God's cultural mandate to 'fill the earth and subdue it' is given to human beings in Genesis 1:28 and reiterated to Noah in Genesis 9:7.4 This is roundly repudiated by the peoples of the earth as they decide to settle on the plain of Shinar to build a tower so that they would *not* be scattered over the globe (11:4).

There is a decidedly universal feel to what is happening. The word 'all' or 'whole' (Hebrew *kol*) appears at a number of points in the narrative. In verse 1, the 'whole earth' is the description of the scope of humanity; whereas, verses 4 and 8 describe the whole earth into which humanity would be distributed. The whole of humanity is referred to in verse 9 and mentioned earlier in verse 6 relating to the sharing of a common language.

In other words, this is an exercise of *collective* rebellion. Austin writes, 'The compiler seemed determined to communicate that all of the people of this period were

---

4   The idea of 'subduing the earth' is an expression of fulfilling his role as God's image-bearer. Thus far from simply *submitting* to nature, as Lewis argued, there is implied a *taming* of nature, for God's glory and mankind's benefit. Because of our sinful nature such a position of trust is taken advantage of, so that exploration of creation can degenerate into exploitation. In this Lewis had a point, which is well illustrated by the Babel episode.

involved as "one" people, a concept that agrees with Genesis' emphasis on the universality of sin.'[5]

The peoples display great technological ingenuity in the building of the tower with bricks utilizing the materials of their environment to create something as strong as stone, but malleable like clay. Cain may have built a city in Genesis 4:17, but that was nothing compared to this latest enterprise. Since then humankind has advanced and appears to be in a position to shape nature rather than be shaped by nature. People can 'boldly go where no man has been before' to use the words of the 'gospel according to Gene Rodenberry' in the 1960's Star Trek series. There is now a tower in this city which people can see for miles and stand gazing at in amazement.

For the Fame of Our Name

We are told that the primary motivation in their attempt to create an architectural superstructure was to make a 'name for themselves,'[6] This forces us to ask: How could such a name be gained? The answer lies in what it is hoped the tower will achieve. Contrary to the common view that

---

5   Austin, *The Tower of Babel in Genesis*, 'To add to this universal scope, the narrative
    includes the word "one"—*echaòd* in Hebrew. In verses 1 and 6, the "oneness" of
    language was highlighted. Verse 6 further emphasized the 'oneness' of the people.
    The idea is not only that all of humanity was involved in the Tower of Babel event,
    but also that they were operating within the confines of a single language. This not
    only re-establishes the universality of the narrative, but also sets the stage for later
    events in the narrative.'

6   The 'name' in Scripture is strongly associated with the identity or the essence of a
    thing, see Craig G. Bartholomew, *The Drama of Scripture: Finding Our Place in the
    Biblical Story* (London: SPCK, 2014).

the Ziggurat was a means by which humans might *ascend* to the heights of heaven, it was seen as a holy place which would bring *God down* from heaven.[7] The assumption is that with the right technique and 'expertise' humankind can domesticate God, enticing him down to dwell among them and so bless them. In the pagan mind it was based on the belief that the gods had needs which humans could meet and as such the Babel account represents a distortion of the nature of God, corrupting his image by reshaping him in *their* image. Having the power to 'bring God down', in more senses than one, is bound to result in a great name for then you appear greater than God himself!

Symptoms of Sin

Here we have testimony to human ingenuity and determination which in this instance, as John Piper argues in *Spectacular Sins*, are outward expressions of two inward sins.[8]

The first sin is the craving for human praise. This doesn't mean it is wrong to praise people. When something has been achieved which is laudable, we should give people their due recognition. But it is when we liven for human praise, and when human praise becomes the force which motivates us that it turns into a form of idolatry.

The second sin is to do with the craving for security—

---

7   John H. Walton, 'Ancient Near Eastern Background Studies', in *Dictionary for Theological Interpretation of the Bible,* ed. by Kevin J. Vanhoozer (Grand Rapids: Baker, 2005), p. 44.

8   See John Piper, *Spectacular Sins,* (Wheaton: Crossway Books, 2008), p. 67.

hence the desire to build the city so that people are not dispersed; as we say, there is 'safety in numbers'. There is nothing wrong in seeking praise or security in themselves, what matters is from *whom* we seek ultimate praise and security. What we have in this account is a society which wants both of those things without God.

Also note the importance language plays. The people see language as a means of *power* to *do* things, not just to *talk about* things. The three fold, 'let us' spoken by humans, mimics God's creative act in making humans in Genesis 1:26. And it is the power of the use of language which God disrupts in an act of judgement and mercy as he 'comes down' by his own volition in verse 5. There is judgement which results in the inability to exercise such power with Promethean pride as God confuses their languages; but also mercy by God's limitation of that power which, because of the wickedness of the human heart, would invariably be abused. Ironically, what was designed to bring fame becomes a symbol of folly, 'Far from being the last word in human culture, it is the ultimate symbol of man's failure when he attempts to go it alone.'[9]

But there is another element of defiance which might be in operation.

Blurring the Boundaries

In the creation account of Genesis 1 God brings order out of chaos by the twofold act of 'separation' (establishing

---

9   Craig Bartholomew, *The Drama of Scripture*. No pn.

boundaries) and 'filling': the separation of light from darkness; water from water, land from sky and the attendant filling: fish, vegetation, animals, heavenly bodies and birds, each suited to its own sphere:

The earth was

shapeless   empty

Day 1
The separation of
Light and darkness.

Day 4
Creation of lights to
rule the day and night.

Day 2
Separation of waters
Form sky and sea.

Day 5
Creation of birds and
fish to fill Sky and sea.

Day 3
Separation of the sea
From the dry land and
the creation of plants.

Day 6
Creation of animals and
humans to fill the land
and eat the plants.

Day 7

In the narrative of Noah and the Flood in Genesis 7 we see those boundaries removed so the world collapses back into a kind of primeval chaos.

The importance of things occupying their rightful place within the bounds *God* has decreed is underscored by the purity laws in Leviticus 11 where the animals are rendered 'clean' according to where they occupy the threefold division of Genesis 1—above, below or dry land—as distinct from the animals which are 'unclean' by virtue of the fact they somehow blur those boundaries (e.g.

animals in the water which do *not* have fins or scales).[10] Far from these laws being arbitrary, they were meant to be daily reminders to God's people that it is *God* who is creator not man; *he* determines the nature of reality, not us. The laws against homosexuality, transvestism and bestiality also stand against such destructive blurring and the deconstructing of the boundaries of creation. Could it therefore not be that by building the tower from the *earth* to the *heavens* , that those boundaries were being further transgressed in an implicit attempt to redefine reality and so usurp God?

The Three 'C's'

There are three ways that the 'hideous strength' attempts to exert itself over and against God which this episode illustrates.

First, there is *communalism*—the group identity and solidarity in rebellion. While the rest of the Genesis' narratives have *individuals* who are identified as playing significant roles, here we have humankind as a *group* acting to the detriment of the individual.

Second, there is *constructionism*, literally in the building of a city and a tower, but also in using language to reshape reality, believing and declaring that we are able to bring God down and so 'de-god' God as it were, who is the

---

10 I am grateful to Steffen Jenkins of UNION for drawing my attention to this. See Mary Douglas, *Purity and Danger: An Analysis of the Concepts of Pollution and Taboo* (London: Routledge paperbacks, 1984) and *Leviticus as Literature* (Oxford: Oxford University Press, 2001).

ultimate reality. It is then a short step from this idolatrous construal to reimagining everything else—which of course the pagan world did by identifying different parts of creation as gods which needed somehow to be controlled.

This is evident in Ancient Egyptian cosmology for example. The Earth, *Geb*, is the god wearing a suit decorated with sheaves of grain adopting a recumbent posture.

Nut is the sky goddess—making an arch of her body over *Geb* and *Shu,* the air. The Sun is the god *Ra* (or *Re*)—a supreme deity in the Egyptian pantheon. His ship rises in the twilight behind *Nut's* legs and then glides down her arms to the place of the dead.

Thirdly, there is *connectivity*. Being in one place and having one language enables the people to connect with each other and so perpetuate their blasphemous ideas and actions even further.

What we have in the Tower of Babel episode is in effect a *rival cosmology* or 'social imaginary' to that of God's; it is an unmaking and a remaking of the world—a blasphemous human 'let us' over and against the holy 'Let Us' of the Triune God.

Chapter 3
What Goes Round Comes Around

LET US NOW TAKE A LOOK AT HOW THAT 'HIDEOUS Strength' has been increasing its grip in the West.

From 'Was-isms' to 'Now-isms'

We saw how <u>for Lewis, the ideology of his day</u>, which he sought to expose and debunk, <u>was naturalistic materialism</u>. <u>One of the main ideologies of our day is a variant of this, namely, neo-Marxism, sometimes called cultural Marxism or libertarian Marxism.</u> The terms can be used interchangeably but for the most part we shall use the term 'cultural Marxism' which, as we shall see, focuses for us <u>the main strategy for bringing about a revolution by changing and capturing the culture of a society</u>.

In order to understand what is 'neo' or 'new' about this

brand of Marxism it might be helpful to provide a brief sketch of classical Marxism from which it originated.

Classical Marxism

Karl Marx (1818–1883) was a former student of the great German idealist philosopher, G.W.F. Hegel (1770–1831). The 'idealism' in Hegel's philosophy was that—at the risk of oversimplification—all reality was the outworking of the Absolute Spirit through nature, history, or human minds. For Hegel religion itself was the 'self-consciousness of God.' (*The Philosophy of Religion*, II). In other words, *all* that we experience is part of the process of a kind of divine evolution which is progressive and inexorable.

There is an important aspect of Hegel's philosophy which has special significance for our understanding of cultural Marxism and many of the things we see and experience in Western Culture. Carl Trueman helpfully summarises this particular aspect,

> [Hegel] forcefully argued that human selves do not exist in isolation as self-conscious beings, but only have self-consciousness as they relate to others. Here is how he expresses it in his Phenomenology of Spirit: "Self-consciousness exists in and for itself when, and by the fact that, it so exists for another; that is, it exists only in being acknowledged." To cut through the jargon and to put this simply, Hegel is saying that we know who we are by the relationship we have to others—our parents,

our siblings, our spouses, our children, our colleagues, and so on.[1]

Marx sought to turn 'Hegel upside down' as he puts it in the preface to his second edition of *Das Kapital* in 1833:

> My dialectic method is not only different from the Hegelian, but is its direct opposite [...] With me [...] the ideal is nothing else than the material world reflected by the human mind, and translated into forms of thought [...] With him it is standing on its head. It must be turned right side up again, if you would discover the rational kernel within the mystical shell.[2]

Marx agreed with Hegel that our identity as human beings was to be construed in terms of our human relationships. However, the nature of those relationships was not determined by ideas or 'Spirit', but by the material, and more specifically, our place in an economy. For Marx the fundamental human problem consisted of two things: oppression and alienation. Oppression resulted from living in a capitalist society which was inherently exploitative and unjust as the ruling class (the *bourgeoisie*) owned the means of production, using and abusing the working class (the *proletariat*) to feather their own nests. The result was that the worker experienced a fourfold alienation, 'first, from the act of production; second, from

---

1   Carl Trueman, 'We All Live In Marx's World Now', https://www.thegospelcoalition. org/reviews/live-marxs-world-now/ [accessed: 18/12/2019]

2   Cited by Robert J. Smith, 'Cultural Marxism: Imaginary Conspiracy or Revolutionary Reality?', p. 438.

the product made; third, from other workers; and fourth from his *Gattungswesen* (species-essence)—i.e., humanity.'[3]

What was Marx's solution? Although for Marx there was an inevitability in the fall of Capitalism and a corresponding rise of Communism through the 'evolution of the material forces of production', nonetheless there is not an *absolute* determinism for man himself who has the capacity to reflect on his situation and so change it and, indeed, transform nature itself.[4] *Violent revolution* was fundamental to bringing about societal change. As Friedrich Engels, co-writer of *The Communist Manifesto*, put it, '[in revolting] the proletarians have nothing to lose but their chains.' Marx elsewhere is more to the point, '[T]here is only one way in which the murderous death agonies of the old society and the bloody birth throes of the new society can be shortened, simplified and concentrated, and that way is revolutionary terror.'[5]

The lens which Marx provided with which to view the world—his 'social imaginary'—was that *everything* is to be seen and understood in terms of economic-social relations such that everything is to be understood politically as part of the class struggle: 'Culture—and everything in it—is a matter of politics, of the overall shape of society, of who oppresses and who is oppressed.'[6] For Marx

---

3 Smith, 'Cultural Marxism: Imaginary Conspiracy or Revolutionary Reality?', p. 439.

4 Brian Magee, 'Karl Marx—Dialogue with Charles Taylor', *Men of Ideas* (London: BBC publications, 1978), p. 45.

5 Cited by Robert Smith, 'Cultural Marxism: Imaginary Conspiracy or Revolutionary Reality?', p. 439.

6 Trueman, 'We All Live in Marx's World Now'.

the primary conflict was between the two classes—the bourgeoisie and the proletariat—with economics being the driving engine. Eventually, the result is alienation, with violent confrontation necessary for social liberation. Cultural Marxism, however, has a significantly different take on things.

Cultural Marxism

Samuel Kronen proposes that cultural Marxism is

> A low resolution interpretation of Marx, packaged in a very particular ideological framework that is applied to all social problems. It is taking his discovery of the conflict between social classes that comes up in the development of advanced civilizations, and assigning the same conflict narrative to all categories of people, whether it be gender, race, class, ethnicity, sexuality, and so on.[7]

The term 'cultural Marxism' itself was apparently coined by the American military theoretician William S. Lind, with its roots lying in the First World War. In the words of one critic, '[cultural Marxism] must be recognised as the most successful political movement of the twentieth century.'[8] One of its modern advocates, Sydney Hook, defines it as,

---

7 Samuel Kronen, 'What Is Cultural Marxism: A Liberal's Critique Of The Radical Left', https://medium.com/@samuelkronen/what-is-cultural-marxism-a-liberals-critique-of-the-radical-left-a01b6e004fb4 [accessed: 18/12/2019]

8 Simon Newman: 'Are We All Cultural Marxists Now?' https://www.conservativehome.com/platform/2006/10/dr_simon_newman.html [accessed 18/12/2019]

[...] a philosophy of human liberation. It seeks to overcome human alienation, to emancipate man from repressive social institutions, especially economic institutions that frustrate his true nature, and to bring him into harmony with himself, his fellow men, and the world around him so that he can overcome his estrangements and express his true essence through creative freedom.[9]

(Remember how in Lewis's story it is one of the aims of N.I.C.E. to liberate men from nature?)

But the liberty which the cultural Marxists have in mind is not the liberty of classical liberalism—equality under the law or equality of opportunity. Unlike the classical Marxist whose main focus was economic inequality, this is an 'equality' cutting across the *whole* of human experience. It was Herbert Marcuse of the Frankfurt School—in his Brandeis University Lecture of 1965—who argued that traditional societies promote what he called a 'repressive tolerance' because they do not deal with the latent inequalities of humans: the fact that some are cleverer, wiser, or harder working than others, who are then to be considered oppressed because of their perceived deficiency.[10] So-called liberal Western societies cannot guarantee equality of outcomes (with people receiving the same wealth, acceptance and prominence).

---

9 Sidney Hook, 'Marxism', in *Dictionary of the History of Ideas*, ed. by Philip P. Wiener (New York: Charles Scribner's, 1973), p. 157.

10 Herbert Marcuse, 'Repressive Tolerance,' in *A Critique of Pure Tolerance, Robert Paul Wolff*, ed. by Barrington Moore Jr. and Herbert Marcuse (Boston: Beacon Press, 1965), pp. 81–117.

At best they could only offer equality of processes such as treating everyone equally under the law. Thus by definition, classically liberal societies were inherently repressive, although they may loudly champion the notion of tolerance. A different society needed to be brought into being to ensure the kind of equality envisaged by Marcuse.

As Andrew Sandlin writes,

> Libertarian Marxism is all about liberating humanity from the social institutions and conditions (like the family and church and business and traditional views and habits and authorities) that prevent the individual from realizing his true self, his true desires and aspirations, from being anything he wants to be—full autonomy [...] Libertarian Marxism is the Marxism of our culture, of our time.[11]

How is such a revolution—one in which 'God is brought down,' and his objective creation to which humanity must conform is discredited—to be achieved?

The Subtle Revolution

To answer this question we turn to the writings of the Italian Neo-Marxist Antonio Gramsci (1891–1937) and his key idea of 'hegemony' (from the Greek *hegemon,* which means 'ruler').[12] This is the process by which a dominant

---

11 P. Andrew Sandlin, 'How Modern Marxism is Libertarian', https://docsandlin. com/2017/08/29/how-modern-marxism-is-libertarian/ [accessed: 18/12/2019]

12 See, George Eaton, 'Why Antonio Gramsci is the Marxist thinker for our times', *New Statesman* (February 2018), https://www.newstatesman.com/culture/

class (think of the directors of N.I.C.E. in Lewis's story) exerts and maintains its influence over people through noncoercive means such as schools, the media and marketing.[13] It works by changing what Peter Berger calls the 'plausibility structures' of a society, that is those background assumptions, beliefs and ways of thinking and acting which are taken as given. It is the presumption which declares 'Of course, everyone nowadays knows that …' (fill in the blanks). The aim is to get people to think and *feel* for themselves that certain values and practices, such as same sex marriage, are common sense, fair or even natural. In short, a different social imaginary is in view.

Gramsci departed from Marx on two essential points.

Firstly, *contra* Marx, Gramsci believed that it was *ideas* and ways of thinking and seeing, that shaped economics rather than the other way around. Secondly, following on from this, change occurs not primarily through a violent overthrow of the ruling elite, but by capturing it at its most culture shaping points, by infiltrating and so overtaking the key culture-making institutions (churches, schools, the media) and civil institutions (the police, law courts, civil service etc.). This process was described by Gramsci as 'becoming State.' The strategy, in short,

---

observations/2018/02/why-antonio-gramsci-marxist-thinker-our-times [accessed: 18/12/2019]

13 The success of establishing hegemony by noncoercive means does not mean that coercion will not be used at some future point when the new hegemony has become more firmly ensconced. People will be forced to accept the 'new plausibility structures' and will be treated as a threat which must be silenced. This is explicit in the work of Herbert Marcuse discussed below.

involves subverting society by changing its *culture* which is brought about by infiltrating its institutions,[14] hence the suitability of describing this brand of Marxism *cultural* Marxism.

> Whereas Marx had written of the 'commanding heights' of the economy—the key industries that essentially controlled the nation's production and distribution— Gramsci's vision was to undermine, and eventually take over, the commanding heights of culture.[15]

Over the last 60 years or so in the West there has effectively occurred the death of one culture, rooted in the Judeo-Christian world view, and the rise of another more secular one. Philip Rieff observes that, 'The death of a culture begins when its normative institutions fail to communicate ideals in ways that remain *inwardly* compelling.'[16] Once the ideology of cultural Marxism becomes 'inwardly compelling' (although you don't scare the horses by *calling* it cultural Marxism, you talk instead about 'equality', 'liberation' and 'tolerance') the revolution is more or less complete. The upshot of this is that if *these* beliefs and practices are considered plausible, *Christian* beliefs and practices become implausible more or less by default, in which case it will not do simply to *argue* for the cogency of the Christian faith for many will think that

---

14 Cited by Smith, 'Cultural Marxism: Imaginary Conspiracy or Revolutionary Reality?', p. 444.

15 Jefrey D. Breshears, 'The Origin of Cultural Marxism and Political Correctness, Part 1' [accessed: 01/01/2020]

16 Philip Rieff, *The Triumph of the Therapeutic: Uses of Faith After Freud* (London: Chatto and Windus, 1966), p. 15.

there is nothing to argue *about*. Many of us don't spend that much time thinking how we might argue against flat earthists—we simply assume they are mistaken, out of touch and an irrelevance; so it is with many people's view of Christianity.

Simon Newman helpfully outlines the 'Gramsci strategy' as composing of three elements, which, he argues, have all but succeeded in the United Kingdom.

The first component is 'positive tolerance'. This he describes as a banding together of all 'Left' forces, defined as those forces seeking destruction of the Enlightenment, whatever their other goals, with the exception of Nazism (thus the requirement that Nazism be defined as a 'Right', or Conservative, force). Critical Theorists, radical feminists, classical Marxists and so on were *not* to criticise each other's positions. (Of course it is often forgotten that the Nazis were 'National *Socialists*').

Secondly, a 'zero tolerance' is required 'for any position taken by 'Right', that is, conservative forces. Marxism adapts the Christian concept of meekness as a virtue so that weakness and oppression (by 'Right' forces) define virtue, but where classical Marxism restricts this to the Proletariat in their relations with Capitalism, cultural Marxism de-emphasises the role of the Proletariat and seeks an ever-expanding coalition of victim groups; racial, ethnic, religious, gender, sex, income, disability, immigrant and so on. The mantle of victimhood sanctifies all, and ultimately becomes so sought after that all seek to attain it.

Both ideas are found in the writings of Marcuse and his notion of 'liberation'. This would not only mean, 'the withdrawal of toleration of speech and assembly from groups and movements which promote aggressive policies, armament, chauvinism, discrimination on the grounds of race and religion', but also the oppression of those who 'oppose the extension of public services, social security, and medical care, etc.'[17] As Marcuse puts it so bluntly, this entails 'intolerance against movements from the Right and toleration of movements from the Left.'[18]

Thirdly, there is what we have already mentioned as central to Gramsci's thesis, namely, capturing the 'commanding heights' of culture. This involves what Rudi Dutschke—'Red Rudi' of the German Student movement of the 1960s—called 'the long march through the institutions'. Newman writes,

> From an initial bulwark in higher education, cultural Marxism in the UK has progressively gained control of thought and instruction in institutions including primary and secondary education, the media, the civil service, law and the legal profession, the government (in 1997), much of the judiciary and most recently the police.[19]

---

17 Herbert Marcuse, "Repressive Tolerance," in *A Critique of Pure Tolerance* ed. by Robert Paul Wolff, Barrington Moore Jr. and Herbert Marcuse. (Boston: Beacon Press, 1965), p. 94.

18 Marcuse, 'Repressive Tolerance', p. 109.

19 Newman: 'Are We All Cultural Marxists Now?'

The New 'Tolerance'

One of the key tools for achieving such a change of perception and feeling amongst members of society is by the destabilisation of language, thus enabling a new language to be devised by which the power of the elite can be exerted. The goal for Marcuse was to, 'break the established universe of meaning'.[20] This lies at the heart of social constructionism (words do not necessarily *refer* to anything, except perhaps to other words in a language matrix (Derrida))[21], but they are *tools*, units of power to be employed deconstructing and reconstructing, creating our own Towers of Babel around which we can rally and 'bring God down'. This involves censoring not just words but *thoughts*. and it is here that the 'hideous strength' is seen at its strongest and most hideous. According to Marcuse cultural subversion 'must begin with stopping the words and images which feed this [opposing] consciousness. To be sure, this is censorship, even pre-censorship.'[22] He writes,

---

20 Marcuse, 'Repressive Tolerance', p. 98.

21 Jacques Derrida (1930–2004) was one of the most prominent 'literary philosophers' of the 20th century, developing a form of linguistic analysis called 'deconstructionism'. As Kevin Vanhoozer notes, 'Where Plato sees signs imitating things, Derrida sees only signs—signs that refer not to some higher realm, only sideways to other signs [...]meaning is not the thing signified, but the endless displacement of one sign by another, a ceaseless play of signs that never come to rest on something in the world.' Kevin J. Vanhoozer, *Is there a meaning in this text? The Bible, the reader and the morality of literary knowledge* (Grand Rapids: Apollos, 1998), p. 61. Here Derrida builds on the earlier Swiss linguist, Ferdinand de Saussure—see Melvin Tinker, *The Bible as Literature: The Implications of Structuralism'* (London: UCCF, 1987).

22 Marcuse, 'Repressive Tolerance', p. 111.

Tolerance [that is neo-Marxist 'tolerance'] cannot be indiscriminate and equal with respect to the contents of expression, neither in word nor in deed; it cannot protect false words and wrong deeds which demonstrate that they contradict and counteract the possibilities of liberation. Such indiscriminate tolerance is justified in harmless debates, in conversation, in academic discussion; it is indispensable in the scientific enterprise, in private religion. But society cannot be indiscriminate where the pacification of existence, where freedom and happiness themselves are at stake: here, certain things *cannot* be said, certain ideas *cannot* be expressed, certain policies *cannot* be proposed, certain behaviour *cannot* be permitted without making tolerance an instrument for the continuation of servitude'. (emphases mine)[23]

Notice all those 'cannots'? Who do you think they are applied to? Mainly people like Christians. This is a new totalitarian-tolerance while all the time masquerading as a new freedom. As such the new tolerance must extinguish the old tolerance and those people and institutions which traditionally espouse it such as the Church. Furthermore, for neo-Marxism to have a *raison d'être* there

must be repressed groups which need liberating. There is an extension of Marx's 'class warfare'. People are required to see themselves as *victims* of the liberal society of which they are a part. Of course there will never be a shortage of victim groups as they can be divided and subdivided *ad nauseum*, hence the breaking down of the sexual identity

---

23 Marcuse, 'Repressive Tolerance', pp. 100–101.

into the sexual alphabet spaghetti which now stands at 'LGBTQIAPK'.[24]

PC or not PC? That is the Question

It is cultural Marxism which lies behind the all-pervading political correctness of our age.[25] Those of both the political right and left acknowledge this. Pat Buchanan of the right wrote, 'Political Correctness is cultural Marxism, a regime to punish dissent and to stigmatize social heresy as the Inquisition punished religious heresy. Its trademark is intolerance.'[26] Similarly from the more liberal publication *Newsweek*,

> PC is, strictly speaking, a totalitarian philosophy [...] Politically, PC is Marxist in origin [...] There are [...] some who recognize the tyranny of PC but see it only as a transitional phase, which will no longer be necessary once the virtues of tolerance are internalized. Does that sound familiar? It's the dictatorship of the proletariat.[27]

There are two notable and concerning features regarding the ideology of political correctness.

First of all there is the assigning of value to people according to their group identity, defined according to

---

24 'Lesbian, gay, bi-sexual, trans, queer, inter-sex, asexual, pansexual and kinky.'
25 This is a term which has had a long association with communism. For example, it is used by Mao Tse Tung in his Little Red Book.
26 Pat Buchanan, *The Death of the West* (Griffin: St Martins Griffin, 2002), p. 89.
27 Cited by Jefrey D. Breshears, *The Origin of Cultural Marxism and Political Correctness*, Part 1 http://www.theareopagus.org/blog/wp-content/uploads/2017/04/Origins-of-Cultural-Marxism-1-Article-Revised.pdf [accessed: 20/12/2019]

broad sociological categories like race, gender, sexual orientation and so on. But such categories are not comparable. Race, such as being ethnically black, is not the same as ideology, such as feminism. Some may consider homosexuality to be a lifestyle choice, others a moral issue, both of which are very different from matters of race and ideology. Furthermore, what is one to do with the mixing of categories, such as being a black, feminist, homosexual? Is one's value as an oppressed minority tripled compared to someone who simply falls into a single category? One would imagine that the proponents of 'intersectionality', (the view which holds that that the overlap of various social identities leads to a certain type of systematic oppression felt by individuals who inhabit more than one of those groups), would answer, 'most certainly'! Is it not also condescending to have, say, a black woman as a token representative of a group simply because of her race and gender, for does this not suggest that 'all black women are the same'?

But there is another downside to such a categorisation of people which is picked up by the former Marxist, David Horowitz:

> By obliterating the particulars and casting parties as genders rather than individuals, the question of guilt and innocence is pre-ordained [...] In identity politics only collective rights matter—not individual rights. What matters is one's membership in a 'victim' group or 'oppressor' group. Membership is based on

characteristics the individual can't change. Identity politics is a politics of hate and a prescription for war.[28]

If one belongs to a designated 'oppressive group', for example, privileged white male, one is 'guilty' simply by virtue of belonging to that group regardless of how one may have acted as an individual. At least if an individual considers the stance or actions he had previously taken were morally wrong, then he can change or to use the religious term, repent. Such a possibility however, is not open to a group, the designated 'oppressor group' must forever be burdened with a stigma so long as it continues to exist.

William Lind is almost apocalyptic in his description of the corrosive effects of political correctness in freedom and democracy,

> For the first time in our history, Americans have to be fearful of what they say, of what they write, and of what they think. They have to be afraid of using the wrong word, a word [considered] offensive or insensitive, or racist, sexist, or homophobic [...]Unless it is defeated, [Political Correctness] will eventually destroy [...] everything that we have ever defined as our freedom, and our culture.[29]

In the second place truth is at a discount. As we have

---

28 David Horowitz, *Dark Agenda: the War to Destroy Christian America* (Boca Raton: Humanix Books, 2018), p. 142.

29 William S. Lind, 'The Origins of Political Correctness.' https://www.academia.org/the-origins-of-political-correctness/ accessed: 20/12/2019

noted with Marcuse, certain truths are to be declared non-truths, subject to social or even state censorship because they hurt people's feelings or are considered intolerant. This means that some groups and individuals are immune from criticism. The 'victim' group cannot be criticized for such criticism is but another evidence of abuse by an oppressor!

The parallels with overt totalitarian regimes are striking ('the Party cannot be wrong').[30] For neo-Marxist György Lukács, the saying of the German nineteenth-century idealist philosopher Gottlieb Fichte is taken as axiomatic to further the revolution, 'If theory conflicts with the facts, so much the worse for the facts.'[31] It is the inability to recognise this feature of cultural Marxism as it works itself out, for example, in the debate on homosexuality in the Church which leads to frustration and failure by conservative Christians. No matter how many Bible texts one might refer to or theological arguments adduced to support the traditional position on the matter, even when backed up by scientific and medical findings, the progressive steam roller has been set in motion and trivial matters such as 'truth' will not be allowed to get in the way. This is tied to another 'given' of Lukács, 'Communist ethics makes it the highest duty to accept the necessity to

---

30 'In the postmodern world, the question is no longer 'Is it true?' but rather 'Whose truth is it?' and 'Which power stands to gain?' As Hitler propaganda minister Joseph Goebbels declared in a foretaste of postmodernism, 'We do not talk to say something but to obtain an effect.' Os Guinness, *Time for Truth: Living in a world of Lies, Hype and Spin* (London: Inter Varsity Press, 2000), p. 13.

31 Quoted by György Lukács, *Tactics and Ethics: Political Writings, 1919–1929* trans. by Michael McColgan; ed. by Rodney Livingstone (London: NLB, 1972), p. 27.

act wickedly.'[32] The progressives play to a different set of
rules and take no hostages.

Critical Theory and the Frankfurt School

In 1923 a week-long symposium was organised by Felix
Weil in Frankfurt, Germany in which they laid out a
vision for a Marxist think-tank and research centre.
The symposium was chaired by the radical Hungarian
Marxist, György Lukács. It was to be modelled after the
Marx-Engels Institute in Moscow. The original name
for the centre was the Institute for Marxism (*Institut
für Marxismus*), but a more innocent sounding title was
subsequently given, 'The Institute for Social Research'
(*Institut für Sozialforschung*). Since that time the ISR has
usually been known simply as the Frankfurt School.

In 1930 Max Horkheimer became the director of the
ISR which is when neo-Marxism was launched in earnest.
Like Gramsci and Lukács before him, Horkheimer
was convinced that the major obstacle to the spread of
Marxism was traditional Western culture with its Judeo-
Christian heritage. Here there developed a revisionist
neo-Marxist interpretation of Western culture under the
rubric, *Critical Theory*, the goal of which according to
William S. Lind 'was not truth but praxis, or revolutionary
action: bringing the current society and culture down

---

32 Cited by Smith, 'Cultural Marxism: Imaginary Conspiracy or Revolutionary
   Reality?', p. 449.

through unremitting, destructive criticism.'[33] 'Truth',
according to this view, was locked into its own particular
point in history and so was historically relative (of course
that would apply to Critical Theory itself a fact which
was conveniently overlooked). Perhaps more to the point
is that members of oppressed groups have special access
to 'the truth' by virtue of their 'life experience', whereas
the oppressors forfeit any such truth claims as they are
blinded by their privilege. So on the one hand there
are the 'oppressed' who are privileged to truth (with
special exemptions) and the 'privileged' who only appeal
to 'objective truth' to further their oppression. This
underscores one of the key elements of Critical Theory,
everything is to be seen through the prism of power.

> Each individual is seen either as oppressed or as an
> oppressor, depending on their race, class, gender,
> sexuality, and a number of other categories. Oppressed
> groups are subjugated not by physical force or even
> overt discrimination, but through the exercise of
> hegemonic power—the ability of dominant groups to
> impose their norms, values, and expectations on society
> as a whole, relegating other groups to subordinate
> positions.[34]

THIS IS WHAT CRT & SOCIAL JUSTICE GROUPS DO : EXERT HEGEMONICAL POWER. DISGUSTING THAT

33 William S. Lind, "Further Readings in the Frankfurt School," in Political Correctness:
   A Short History of an Ideology. www.freecongress.org [accessed: 20/12/2019]
34 Neil Shenvi and Pat Sawyer, 'The Incompatibility of Critical Theory and
   Christianity', *The Gospel Coalition* (2019), https://www.thegospelcoalition.org/
   article/incompatibility-critical-theory-christianity/ [accessed: 19/12/2019]

THEY ACCUSE OTHERS OF DOING WHAT THEY DO — THEY'RE PROJECTING.

Weapons of Mass Deception

A key element of Critical Theory was the integration of Marxism with Darwinism and Freudianism. Drawing in Freudianism was quite a bold move for the Frankfurt School since, according to Breshears,

> Philosophically, Freudianism was inherently counterrevolutionary in that it discounted the primacy of economics in human social evolution in favour of liberation through psychoanalysis and the release of libidinal impulses. Rather than a violent external revolution that immediately liberated the masses, the Freudian revolution was peaceful, deliberative, individual and internal.[35]

Nonetheless, great potential was seen in harnessing Freudianism for their cause. According to Horkheimer and his fellow scholars, bourgeois society is inherently sexually repressed, which is a major factor in neurosis and other forms of mental illness. 'They believed,' as Breshears makes clear, 'that a revolutionary, post-capitalist and post-Christian society could liberate humanity from this repression, so sexual liberation from the restrictions of a patriarchal society was a major theme in their ideology.'[36]

Many years earlier, Lukács' chief goal was the destruction of traditional sexual morality and the family.

---

35 Jefrey D. Breshears, 'The Origins of Cultural Marxism and Political Correctness, Part 2', http://www.theareopagus.org/blog/wp-content/uploads/2017/04/Origins-of-Cultural-Marxism-2-Article-Revised, p. 30. [accessed: 20/12/2019]

36 Breshears, 'The Origins of Cultural Marxism and Political Correctness', p. 31.

He believed that he could achieve both in one stroke by introducing radical sex education into every Hungarian school. According to William Borst,

> Hungarian children learned the subtle nuances of
> free love, sexual intercourse, and the archaic nature
> of middle-class family codes, the obsolete nature of
> monogamy, and the irrelevance of organised religion,
> which deprived man of pleasure.[37]

What was then considered radical (and short lived as it happened) is now being introduced into primary schools throughout the United Kingdom, another sign that cultural Marxism has all but won the day regardless which political party is in government.

Both Eric Fromm and Wilhelm Reich re-worked Freudianism into the neo-Marxist ideology. Fromm argued that sexual orientation is merely a social construct, that there are no innate differences between men and women, and furthermore that sexuality and gender roles are socially determined. It was Reich who coined the term 'the sexual revolution' (the title of his 1936 book) and contended that the innate sexual impulse should be liberated from artificial and man-made moral restrictions.

But perhaps more than any other member of the Frankfurt School it was Herbert Marcuse who was to have the most far-reaching influence in this aspect of the neo-Marxist ideology. In *Eros and Civilization* (1955) he

---

37 William A. Borst, *The Scorpion and the Frog: A Natural Conspiracy* (Bloomington: Xlibris, 2004), p. 105.

sought to bring together neo-Marxism with a version
of neo-Freudianism in order to turn the power of the
libido into a revolutionary force.[38] He called for the
throwing off of all traditional values and sexual restraints
in favour of 'polymorphous perversity' a term borrowed
from Freud.[39] The very idea of marital love and fidelity
was considered by Marcuse to be counter-revolutionary.
Although cultural change was the ultimate goal, Marcuse
understood the tactical appeal of the pleasure principle.
For as we are often reminded, 'sex sells,' and it sells politics
too. What better way to recruit revolutionaries than to
convince them that sexual promiscuity is a sure way to
bring about the revolution? It comes as no surprise that
the phrase 'Make Love not War' is credited to Marcuse,
for within the cultural Marxist paradigm this is a more
effective weapon to utilise to bring about the downfall of a
civilisation than any bomb (as Freud realised, see previous

---

38 Herbert Marcuse, *Eros and Civilization: A Philosophical Inquiry into Freud,* (Boston:
   Beacon Press: 1974 [1955]).

39 Robert Smith makes an important observation which shows how the ideas of one
   man can be twisted to further the agenda of another, 'Given its Freudian origins, it's
   important to understand what Freud himself meant by this expression. He explains
   as follows: 'What makes an infant characteristically different from every other stage
   of human life is that the child is polymorphously perverse, is ready to demonstrate
   any kind of sexual behaviour, with any kind of pleasure, without any kind of
   restraint.' But the child is not meant to stay like this, said Freud. Indeed, maturation
   and "civilization" emerge only after such polymorphous perversity is restrained
   and responsibly re-channelled. Moreover, in Freud's mind, such restraint and
   re-channelling are profoundly necessary; for heterosexual procreation is necessary for
   the continuation of our race, and so heterosexual coupling is essential for civilization
   itself.' 'Cultural Marxism: Imaginary Conspiracy or Revolutionary Reality?', p. 452.

footnote)40 Dinesh D'Souza notes in *What's so great about Christianity?* the centrality of this tactic by quoting a neo-Marxist, 'Against the power of religion we employ an equal if not greater power—the power of hormones.'41

In For The Long Haul

For the members of the Frankfurt school, accomplishing such a revolution would involve infiltrating the key institutions, not least the educational establishments (the parallels with N.I.C.E. are self-evident as it occupies the grounds within an old university).42 It was assumed that

---

40 This is not to say that Marcuse was not in favour of violent revolution to augment indoctrination. The philosopher Brian Magee speaking of the revival of Marxism in the West writes, 'This culminated in 1968, the year which saw the high point of student violence all over Europe and the United States, and looked to some people for a moment, in Paris, as if it might even come near to a genuine revolution. The would-be revolutionaries of that day proclaimed one man more than any others as their political mentor: Marcuse.' *Men of Ideas* (London: BBC publications, 1978), p. 62.

41 It may be added that it is not coincidental that sex is often linked to religion in paganism, both old and new thus creating a 'double power'. See Rahnuma e-books collection http://ebooks.rahnuma.org/religion/ [accessed: 01/01/2020]

42 When Hitler and the Nazi Party came to power in Germany in 1933, the Frankfurt Institute for Social Research was shut down 'for tendencies hostile to the state.' In previous years the ISR had developed contacts with prominent Americans associated with the University of Columbia in New York. When Horkheimer visited the U.S. in May, 1934, he was received by Columbia's president, Nicholas Murray Butler.

Butler offered the ISR official affiliation with the university, including offices and classrooms in one of the university's buildings. The bitter irony is that while the United States was providing sanctuary for Horkheimer and his associates they were working to undermine its democratic institutions. Its relocation and development was only possible through the funding from the Rockefeller Foundation, Columbia Broadcasting System (CBS), the International Labour Organization, the American Jewish Committee and the Jewish Labour Committee, and the Hacker Institute.

there would be a commitment to the *long term*, or 'the long march through the institutions'—a reference to Mao Zedong's Long March to eventual victory in the Chinese Civil War.

This is how Breshears describes the different stages in the 'long march' as it worked itself out in the United States:

> Throughout the 1960s, with the escalation of the Vietnam War, many college and university graduates enrolled in master's programs in hopes of evading the draft, and some of the most radical eventually earned Ph.D.'s with the intention of fundamentally transforming American society through the education system. (Of all the Ph.D. degrees granted by American universities in the 110 years between 1860 and 1970, half were granted in the 1960s.) Others opted to avoid the draft by enrolling in seminary and becoming ministers in liberal Protestant denominations or priests in the Roman Catholic Church. By the mid-to-late 1970s many of these former student radicals were moving into positions as junior faculty and administrators, and by the early 1980s they were firmly entrenched in most universities and attaining tenure. Gradually, liberal arts faculties became more radical as Neo-Marxists began replacing older New Deal liberals who retired, and over time a rigid left-wing ideology prevailed in many departments [...] Likewise, just as former Sixties activists came to dominate in higher education, they moved into key positions of influence in the mainstream media—radio, television, and print media.

[Handwritten marginal annotations: "THE UNIVERSITY" bracketing the first portion, and "THE CHURCH" bracketing the seminary/priests portion.]

As their cultural influence and power increased over time, they grew bolder and more aggressive.[43]

A similar observation of the overwhelming influence of cultural Marxism has been made more recently by Galen Watts:

Since the 1960s, cultural studies has morphed into a vast field of scholarship, characterized by theories and methods as diverse as critical sociology, postmodernism, post-structuralism, feminist and queer theory, post-colonial scholarship, affect theory, as well as literary criticism. Thinkers as diverse as sociologist Pierre Bourdieu, philosopher and historian Michel Foucault, gender theorist Judith Butler, psychoanalyst Jacques Lacan, and post-colonial thinker Edward Said are now accepted as part of the Cultural Studies canon. Although it would be doing an injustice to the diversity of these thinkers and the field of Cultural Studies as a whole to characterize them as merely 'Culturally Marxist,' their scholarship today can be understood as espousing the Cultural Marxism's basic theoretical presuppositions [...] Of course, Cultural Studies is not the sole field in which Cultural Marxism [...] is found. It is also taught in departments as diverse as anthropology, sociology, gender and women's studies, education, history, geography, and philosophy. Accordingly, it is fair to say that Cultural Marxism, understood as a certain kind of social theory, is relatively commonplace in the humanities and

---

43 Breshears, *The Origins of Cultural Marxism and Political Correctness*, pp. 34–35.

social sciences, and also within the wider culture— that is, it has become a common lens through which many on the Left understand society. This does not mean, of course, that most progressives today have a comprehensive understanding of Gramsci's thought, or that they are committed to the project of liberation as articulated by the Frankfurt School; it means only that the theoretical presupposition that I outlined earlier has seeped into the wider progressive milieu so such an extent that is often taken for granted.[44]

Perhaps it is worth mentioning at this point that those, like Jordan Peterson, who seek to expose the all-pervading influence of cultural Marxism, are sometimes derisively dismissed as buying into a 'conspiracy theory', as if there is a carefully co-ordinated SPECTRE-like international group which meets in a clandestine manner plotting the downfall of the capitalist West. I am not aware of any reputable writer who is suggesting any such conspiracy.[45] However, given the widespread and strategic occupation of cultural Marxist ideas and methods in key institutions— such as academia, the media and different levels of government—it can be said that there *is* a conspiracy in the same sense as when we speak of 'everything conspiring to make a situation worse.' There need not be an overt pact made between those who occupy such positions of

44 Galen Watts, 'Cultural Marxism' Explained and Re-Evaluated', https://quillette. com/2018/06/23/cultural-marxism-explained-and-re-evaluated/ [accessed: 15/12/2019]

45 Smith notes, 'for something to be a conspiracy it needs to be a secret. But there never was anything remotely secret about the work of the Frankfurt school.' 'Cultural Marxism: Imaginary Conspiracy or Revolutionary Reality?', p. 462.

power who promote cultural Marxist values (and let us not forget those whom Lenin called 'useful idiots') for there to be a *tacit* agreement that *this* is the social imaginary they want to see operating in the West.

"If you do not agree it is because you are a fascist!"

By a semantic sleight of hand, those who appear critical of the neo-Marxist agenda are labelled fascist, a move originally made in 1950 by Theodor Adorno in his book, *The Authoritarian Personality.*[46] He began this work in 1923 and claimed to identify a 'new anthropological type', an authoritarian personality which itself was the product of capitalism, Christianity, conservatism, the family, and sexual repression.

Adorno constructed an *F-scale* (Fascist-Scale), a rating system based on nine personality variables. These are the following traits:

1. Conventionalism. Rigid adherence to conventional middle-class values.

2. Authoritarian submission. A submissive and uncritical attitude toward authority figures.

3. Authoritarian aggression. The inclination to apply or enforce conventional values on others, punishing those who don't conform.

---

46 T.W. Adorno, *The Authoritarian Personality (Studies in Prejudice)* (New York: W.W. Norton & Co, 1994).

4. Anti-intraception. Opposition to the subjective, the imaginative, or the intuitive.

5. Superstition and stereotypy. The belief in the supernatural or mystical determinism, and the disposition to think in rigid categories (i.e., racial, ethnic and gender prejudice).

6. Power and toughness. A preoccupation with dominance-submission, strong-weak, leader follower; identification with power figures; exaggerated assertion of strength and toughness.

7. Destructiveness and cynicism. Generalized hostility and the tendency to vilify others.

8. Projectivity. The disposition to believe that wild and dangerous things go on in the world.

9. Sex. An exaggerated concern with conventional sexual morality and a preoccupation with other people's sexual practices.[47]

This is a tactical definition which immediately puts Christians in their place as die hard fascists![48] It would be tempting to play Adorno at his own game and produce an *M-scale* by simply modifying the above traits in a different direction (e.g. Unconventionlism. A childish and unthinking adherence to the latest popular trend. Authoritarian aggression. The inclination to apply or

---

[47] Breshears, *The Origins of Cultural Marxism and Political Correctness*, p. 36.

[48] The term 'tactical definition' was coined by C.S. Lewis, and is one in which a term is so defined as to guarantee the conclusion required. (Lewis, *A Study in Words*)

enforce unconventional values on others), but this achieves very little except to expose the fallacious logic and propagandistic nature of the neo-Marxist enterprise.

The stigmatising of opponents has now become a classic radical tactic which is the thirteenth rule in Saul Alinsky's *Rules for Radicals*: 'Pick the target, freeze it, personalise it, and polarise it.'[49] Those who oppose you are to be personally attacked in such a way that they are cut off from any form of sympathy and so support. The presentation of the progressives opponents as some 'phobe' or other, 'homophobe, Xenophobe, Islamophobe' etc. is an example of this. 'They're not just good-but-misguided people whose religious convictions have led them to a contrasting viewpoint, they are bad people possessed by irrational fears of 'the others' because they are different.'[50]

Bulverism for Today

What this affords is an example of what C.S. Lewis dubbed '*Bulverism*' whereby an opponent's belief is assumed to be wrong and credited as being the result of some bias and thus can be discounted once it has been

---

49 Saul Alinsky, *Rules for Radicals* (New York: Vintage, 1989), p. 130.

50 Horowitz, *Dark Agenda,* p. 164. He goes on to write, 'According to the left, in other words, people who oppose abortion and same-sex marriage have a kind of mental illness. They are not reasonable people, and their thoughts are not rational thoughts. These ritualistic indictments of the sanity of political opponents destroy the fabric of America's pluralism, which requires a respect for opposing views and a search for compromise. Calling critics 'phobic' is a rationale for denying their First Amendment rights. Shouts of 'No free speech for homophobes or Islamophobes' are already heard from leftists on college campuses. Or, to put them all in one fearful basket: 'No free speech for fascists.' pp. 164–165.

discredited.[51] <u>The reasons for an opponent's position do not then need to be considered. In fact it is to neo-Marxism's advantage that one does not draw people's attention to reasons, for then their own position might be examined and found wanting while the alternative is found strong and compelling</u>.

This is how Lewis describes what happens:

The Freudians have discovered that we exist as bundles of complexes […] Nowadays the Freudian will tell you to go and analyse the hundred: you will find that they all think Elizabeth [I] a great queen because they all have a mother-complex. Their thoughts are psychologically tainted at the source […] Now this is obviously great fun; but it has not always been noticed that there is a bill to pay for it. There are two questions that people who say this kind of thing ought to be asked. The first is, are all thoughts thus tainted at the source, or only some? The second is, does the taint invalidate the tainted thought—in the sense of making it untrue—or not? If they say that all thoughts are thus tainted, then, of course, we must remind them that Freudianism and Marxism are as much systems of thought as Christian theology […] The Freudian and Marxian are in the same boat with all the rest of us, and cannot criticize us from outside. They have sawn off the branch they were sitting on. If, on the other hand, they say that the taint need not invalidate their thinking, then neither need it invalidate ours. In which case they

51 C.S Lewis, 'Bulverism', *First and Second Things* (London: Fount, 1985 [1942]).

have saved their own branch, but also saved ours along with it.[52]

This is now a standard tactic used against those who would stand opposed to cultural Marxism and the various sub-ideologies it has spawned. <u>Forget argument and reason, assume your opponent is wrong or stupid (or both) and explain his ideas away by appealing to pseudoscience.</u> This happened to me a few years ago when I was in Jerusalem at the Global Anglican Future Conference (GAFCON). During the conference there was a large gay pride event taking place down the road from where we were meeting and I was invited by the BBC to attend and debate with one of its leaders. The interview appeared on BBC World News. As you can imagine I received a fair amount of correspondence as a result, and not all of it was favourable! One of the most interesting letters I received was from someone who was gay saying that my objection to homosexual practice must be because *I* was repressing a latent homosexuality of my own. This is pure Bulverism. He could not or didn't want to concede that I might have reasons to think homosexual practice was wrong and stands as an example of disordered sexuality—so there must be some psychological explanation for my position, namely, I must be gay but refusing to acknowledge it.[53]

---

52 Lewis, 'Bulverism', pp. 13–18.

53 To charge someone who speaks out against homosexuality as themselves being a repressed homosexual is a tactic explicitly suggested by Marshall Kirk and Hunter Madsen, in *After the Ball: How America Will Conquer Its Fear and Hatred of Gays in the 90's* (New York: Plume Books, 1989).

This is one instance of the dominant social imaginary at work which Christians must understand if they are not to be taken captive by it and if they are to be equipped to protest against it:

> For over a hundred years now, modern culture has been secularising the social imagination. The so-called masters of suspicion, Marx, Freud, Nietzsche, have explained away Christianity in terms of ideology, wish-fulfilment, and the will to power, all terms that modern people readily understand. Modern and postmodern culture has cultivated ways of living and seeing the world that simply left God out of the picture. Yet even a secular culture's pictures are powerful means of spiritual formation.[54]

Who Cares?

We can all be selective of the kind of evidence we wish to accept or ignore depending upon whether it will support or contradict our cherished theory. But there comes a point when such selectivity is so ingrained, and integrity so compromised, that the position of those committed to their cause at any cost brings into question their whole enterprise. This is certainly the case with the members of the Frankfurt School, especially as many of them sheltered in a democratic country, the USA—a country which they then sought to undermine. Here is Roger Scruton's assessment:

---

54 Kevin J Vanhoozer, *Hearers and Doers,* p. 106.

By constantly notching up the critique of American capitalism and its culture, and making only muted or dismissive references to the real nightmare of communism, those thinkers showed their profound indifference to human suffering and the unserious nature of their prescriptions. Adorno does not explicitly say that the 'alternative' to the capitalist system and the commodity culture is Utopia. But that is what he implies. And Utopia is not a real alternative. Hence his alternative to the unreal freedom of the consumer society is itself unreal—a mere noumenon whose only function is to provide a measure of our defects. And yet he was aware that there was an actual alternative on offer and that it involved mass murder and cultural annihilation. For Adorno to dismiss this alternative merely as the 'totalitarian' version of the same 'state capitalism' that he had witnessed in America was profoundly dishonest.[55]

A New Dark Age?

At a fundamental level the dominant and dominating social imaginary most people are operating with (even some Christians unknowingly) is a Marxist one. Simon Newman asks, 'Are we all cultural Marxists now?'[56] Carl

---

55 Roger Scruton, *Fools, Frauds and Firebrands: Thinkers of the New Left* (London: Bloomsbury, 2015), pp.143–144.

56 The tentative answer he gives is that not only has it infected *all* the major cultural institutions, not least the BBC, but all the major political parties too, mooting the possibility that Cameron Conservatism is cultural Marxist Conservatism!

Trueman is more definite, declaring that, 'We all live in Marx's world now'.[57]

We have already seen how Trueman sees Karl Marx recasting Hegel's thesis that we all find our identity in social relationships, and concludes that,

> Culturally speaking, Marx did win—because his vision of a society where everything's political is our world. From cake-baking to what consenting adults do in the privacy of their own bedrooms, from the gendered membership of school sports teams to the ordination requirements of a church to the casting of an actor in a movie, everything has taken on universal political significance. This is now part of the intuitive way in which we all think about society—whether we're on the right or the left. Once one side decides, for example, that the Boy Scouts needs to admit girls in order to break down gender inequalities, then those who oppose this change aren't acting in a politically neutral way. They too are taking a political stand.

Significantly he writes, 'We live in Marx's world—a world where the cultural imagination is gripped by the idea that everything is political.'[58] This is another way of saying that Marxism is *the* social imaginary of our day.

Michael Minnicino assesses the impact of the Frankfurt School over the past seventy-five years and offers a possible

---

57 Carl Trueman, 'We All Live In Marx's World Now', https://www.thegospelcoalition. org/reviews/live-marxs-world-now/ Accessed: 19/12/2019.

58 *Ibid.*

solution to reverse the damage that has been done to Western culture. He warns if America and the West continue down the road to self-destruction, it could very well usher in a dreadful new Dark Age in human history,

> The principles through which Western Judeo-Christian civilization was built, are now no longer dominant in our society; they exist only as a kind of underground resistance movement. If that resistance is ultimately submerged, then the civilization will not survive—and in our era of pandemic disease and nuclear weapons, the collapse of Western civilization will very likely take the rest of the world with it to Hell. The way out is to create a Renaissance. If that sounds grandiose, it is nonetheless what is needed. A renaissance means, to start again: to discard the evil, inhuman, and just plain stupid, and to go back hundreds or thousands of years to the ideas which allow humanity to grow in freedom and goodness. Once we have identified those core beliefs, we can start to rebuild civilization.[59]

Talk of a renaissance might grate with some Christians; surely it would be better to speak of reformation or revival? Os Guinness makes a reasoned plea for the use of the phrase.[60] He argues for a Christian renaissance, pointing out that the term 'is simply the French word for

---

59 Michael J. Minnicino, *The New Dark Age* https://archive.org/stream/ TheNewDarkAgeTheFrankfurtSchoolAndPoliticalCorrectness/ The+New+Dark+Age+-+The+Frankfurt+School+and+Political+Correctness_djvu.txt [accessed: 19/12/2019]

60 Os Guinness, *Renaissance: The Power of the Gospel However Dark the Times* (Illinois: Inter Varsity Press, 2014).

rebirth, and its deepest roots—and fulfilment—all the way back to Jesus himself and to his night-time conversation with Nicodemus. Rebirth is essentially a Christian notion.' He goes on,

> But the term itself is not what matters [...] what matters is that it is a movement led by the Spirit of God, which involves God's people returning to the ways of God and so demonstrating in our time the kingdom of God, and not in word only but in power and with the plausibility of community expression.[61]

What this might look like will be taken up in a later chapter. Suffice to say that the 'hideous strength' is abroad and the church needs to wake up to the fact as the darkness begins to draw in even closer.

Reimagining the World

As we have seen, by their actions the people of Babel revealed their view of God, the world, and how God was supposed to relate to the world (what we might call their cosmology) which was at variance with Genesis 1 and 2. Similarly today godless views of humanity and the world are being constructed (even within the church) which are diametrically opposed both to God's general and special revelation. Perhaps nowhere is this seen most sharply than in the area of the gay and transgender debate.

---

61 Guinness, *Renaissance: The Power of the Gospel However Dark the Times*, p. 29.

Chapter 4
The Gender Agenda

THE UNDERLYING NATURE OF THE PRESENT CLASH between the Judeo-Christian world view and the dominant secularist view in the West is underscored by Rod Dreher's subtitle to his article, 'Sex After Christianity: Gay marriage is not just a social revolution but a cosmological one.'[1]

Dreher draws attention to a cover story in a 1993 copy of *The Nation*, which said that if the gay-rights cause was to succeed, it would have to design 'a complete cosmology.' As Dreher puts it, 'the gay-rights cause has succeeded precisely because the Christian cosmology has dissipated in the mind of the West.' Summarizing this 'new' cosmology, he writes: 'To be modern is to believe in one's individual desires as the locus of authority

---

1 Rod Dreher, 'Sex After Christianity: Gay marriage is not just a social revolution but a cosmological one.' http://www.theamericanconservative.com/articles/sex-after-christianity/ [accessed: 19/12/2019]

<u>and self-definition</u>.' Dreher points out that <u>Christians have tended to approach the issue of homosexuality as a moral issue (which it is) but have failed to see it as a cosmological issue, a redefining and reconfiguring of reality—a new Babel</u>.

Having a Ball?

The employment of Gramscian strategy is very much in evidence in Marshall Kirk and Hunter Madsen's *After the Ball: How America Will Conquer its Fear and Hatred of Gays in the 90s*.[2] Al Mohler writes,

> The spectacular success of the homosexual movement stands as one of the most fascinating phenomena of our time. In less than two decades, homosexuality has moved from 'the love that dares not speak its name,' to the centre of America's public life. The homosexual agenda has advanced even more quickly than its most ardent proponents had expected, and social change of this magnitude demands some explanation.[3]

---

2   Marshall Kirk and Hunter Johnson, *After the Ball: How America Will Conquer Its Fear and Hatred of Gays in the 90's* (New York: Plume Books, 1989). The book began life as an article in November 1987 entitled 'The Overhauling of Straight America' in *Guide* Magazine, with advice such as this: 'While we're storming the battlements with salvos of ink, we should also warm the mainstream up a bit with a subtle national campaign on highway billboards. In simple bold print on dark backgrounds, a series of unobjectionable messages should be introduced: IN RUSSIA, THEY TELL YOU WHAT TO BE. IN AMERICA WE HAVE THE FREEDOM TO BE OURSELVES … AND TO BE THE BEST. … or PEOPLE HELPING INSTEAD OF HATING—THAT'S WHAT AMERICA IS ALL ABOUT.'

3   Al Mohler, 'After the Ball—Why the Homosexual Movement Has Won', http://www.freerepublic.com/focus/religion/1147428/posts[accessed: 18/12/2019]

He rightly draws attention to the influence of this book in providing part of the answer.

Kirk and Madsen (both Harvard graduates and 'Madmen'—Maddison Avenue advertizing consultants) combined psychiatric and public relations expertise in devising their strategy. Kirk, a researcher in neuropsychiatry, and Madsen, a public relations consultant, argued that homosexuals must change their presentation to the heterosexual community if real success was to be made. They understood how to change completely a culture's view of the gay issue within a generation, although few believed it to be possible at the time. 'First you get your foot in the door', they write,

> By being as similar as possible; then, and only then— when your one little difference is finally accepted—can you start dragging in your other peculiarities, one by one. You hammer in the wedge narrow end first. As the saying goes, 'Allow the camel's nose beneath your tent and his whole body will soon follow.'[4]

Three ploys are to be taken up, they argue.

1. Desensitization: 'To desensitize straights, Homosexuals inundate them with a conscious flood of Homosexual related advertizing, presented in the least offensive fashion. If straights can't shut the shower off, they may at least eventually get used to being wet.'[5]

---

4   Kirk and Madsen, 'After the Ball', p. 146.
5   Kirk and Madsen, 'After the Ball', p. 149.

2. <u>Jamming</u>: Jamming is <u>more active and aggressive</u> <u>than desensitization, aiming to produce 'emotional</u> <u>dissonance' whereby people will for a while still have</u> <u>their previous feelings of revulsion but which are</u> <u>brought into conflict with new feelings of sympathy</u> <u>if not empathy.</u> <u>Propaganda is to be used whereby</u> <u>those who are traditional in their stance on the gay</u> <u>issue are portrayed as loud mouthed homophobes—</u> <u>rednecks of a Ku Klux Klan stripe</u> (and no one wants to be associated with them, <u>thus creating a feeling</u> <u>of shame)</u>, and such people should be shown to be disapproved of <u>which in turn will 'cause them to</u> <u>keep their heads down and mouths shut.'</u>[6] That is exactly what is happening.

3. <u>Conversion:</u> This is the ultimate goal. Kirk and Madsen say that if desensitization lets the watch run down, and jamming throws sand in the works, conversion reverses the spring so that the hands run backward:[7]

   <u>Conversion of the average American's emotions, mind,</u> <u>and will, through a planned psychological attack, in the</u> <u>form of propaganda fed to the nation via the media.</u> We mean 'subverting' the mechanism of prejudice to our own ends—using the very process that made America hate us, to turn their hatred into warm regard.[8]

---

6 Kirk and Madsen, 'After the Ball', especially pp. 151–152.

7 Kirk and Madsen, 'After the Ball', p. 154.

8 Kirk and Madsen, 'After the Ball', p. 153–154.

It is regarded as legitimate to use ads which are lies to achieve this end:

> It makes no difference that the ads are lies; not to us, because we're using them to ethically good effect, to counter negative stereotypes that are every bit as much lies, and far more wicked ones; not be bigots, because the ads will have their effect on them whether they believe them or not.[9]

Goebbels Would Be Proud

Propaganda is seen as key to achieving this. The authors point out three characteristics which distinguish propaganda from other modes of communication which contribute to its sinister reputation.

1. Relies on emotional manipulation—through desensitization, jamming and conversion.

2. Uses lies

3. Is subjective and one-sided.

This, however, is deemed necessary to 'win the peace campaign', by telling the gay side of the story as movingly as possible. 'In the battle for hearts and minds, effective propaganda knows enough to put its best foot forward. This is what our own media campaign must do.'[10]

What is actually involved in portraying gay men

---

9   Kirk and Madsen, 'After the Ball', p. 154.
10 Kirk and Madsen, 'After the Ball', pp. 162–163.

and women not only as equal, but as being superior to straights? William Jasper tells us,

> This involves both publicizing an historical "honour roll of prominent gay or bisexual men and women," including "suspected 'inverts'" from "Socrates to Eleanor Roosevelt", and lining up celebrity endorsements. The past few years have witnessed a politically correct stampede of politicians, entertainers, authors, and intellectuals into the "pro-gay" camp, a host of celebs pouring out of the closets, and an avalanche of movies and television programs with homosexual, lesbian, and transvestite characters and themes. Singers Elton John, Boy George, K.D. Lang, Janis Ian, and Melissa Etheridge openly proclaim their "gay" identities. Homosexual movie/record mogul David Geffen (the "G" in SKG Dreamworks, with Steven Spielberg and Jeffrey Katzenberg) lavishes millions of dollars on homosexual causes. Geffen, together with Fox TV founder Barry Diller, Hollywood power broker Sandy Gallin, designer Calvin Klein, and a close group of homosexual and pro-homosexual friends, comprise what has been dubbed the Velvet Mafia, which has boosted the queer content of films and television programming and helped to line up stars such as Oprah Winfrey, Madonna, Tom Hanks, Sharon Stone, Magic Johnson, Barbra Streisand, Ted Danson, and a legion of others to endorse "gay rights" or raise funds for homosexual causes. One measurement of the magnitude of their baleful influence can be seen in the willingness of traditionally macho-male stars Patrick

Swayze and Wesley Snipes to take roles as prancing
transvestites in the drag-queen comedy, *To Wong Foo,
Thanks For Everything, Julie Newmar,* or of Tom Selleck
and Kevin Kline to do the homosexual kissing scene in
the blatant, gay agitprop "comedy," *In and Out.*[11]

With friends like these one can afford to confront one's
perceived enemies.

The gloves are off with regards to the Church, which
is seen as one of the main bastions of resistance to the
gay movement. What is to be done? 'Gays can use
talk to muddy the moral waters, that is, to undercut
the rationalizations that "justify" religious bigotry and
to jam some of its psychic rewards.' And to 'portray
such institutions as antiquated backwaters, badly out
of step with the times and with the latest findings of
psychology.'[12]

This is classic Gramsci. Writing of Gramsci's strategy to
destroy all hierarchies, Smith observes that

The goal here is not merely a *flattening* of the
system, but a *flipping* of the system; the creation of
what Gramsci called a 'periphery-centred society.' In
other words, insiders must be turned into outsiders
and underdogs into overlords. Likewise, oppressors

11   William F. Jasper 'The Queering of America', *New American*, (2015), https://www.
     thenewamerican.com/culture/faith-and-morals/item/14947-the-queering-of-america
     [accessed: 20/12/2019].

12   Jasper, 'The Queering of America', p. 179.

must now be oppressed and those who were formerly privileged must have their privileges taken away.[13]

This, in part, is achieved not by an all-out assault (which Kirk and Marsden warn against—a perpetual 'Stonewalling'—referring to the original riots of 1969), but by seduction: 'Gramsci means to replace Western culture by subverting it, by doing what it takes to compel it to redefine itself, rather than picking fights with it.'[14] GENIUS. AND EVIL.

As Mohler observes:

> A quick review of the last 15 years demonstrates the incredible effectiveness of this public relations advice. The agenda set out by Kirk and Madsen led to nothing less than social transformation. By portraying themselves as mainstream Americans seeking nothing but liberty and self-fulfilment, homosexuals redefined the moral equation. Issues of right and wrong were isolated as outdated, repressive, and culturally embarrassing. Instead, the assertion of "rights" became the hallmark of the public relations strategy [...] The advice offered by Marshall Kirk and Hunter Madsen is nothing less than a manifesto for moral revolution. A look back at this strategy indicates just how self-consciously the homosexual movement advanced its cause by following this plan.[15]

---

13 Smith, 'Cultural Marxism: Imaginary Conspiracy or Revolutionary Reality?', p. 444.

14 Angelo M. Codevilla, 'The Rise of Political Correctness,' *Claremont Review of Books* (Fall 2016), p. 40.

15 Mohler, 'After the Ball—Why the Homosexual Movement Has Won'.

The Persuaders

A number of years ago Os Guinness commented:

> <u>Christians are always more culturally short-sighted than</u>
> <u>they realise.</u> They are often unable to tell, for instance,
> where their Christian principles leave off and their
> cultural perspectives begin. What many of them fail to
> ask themselves is, 'where are we coming from and what
> is our own context?'[16]

That is certainly the case when we consider the cultural
shaping that has been taking place by the gay movement.
If Christians think they are not being influenced by the
kind of marketing techniques which the gay lobby is called
to use by Kirk and Madsen, they simply need to watch the
PBS 'Frontline' documentary *The Persuaders*. Kathryn C.
Montgomery, former Professor of Communications at the
University of California, writes:

> Although a number of lobby groups have campaigned
> for exposure on the airwaves, the gay lobby has been
> by far the most organized and best coordinated,
> soon gaining a reputation as 'the most sophisticated
> and successful advocacy group operating in network
> television.'[17]

All the main cultural transformers have been brought to
bear to achieve this revolution. In addition to advertising,

---

16 Os Guinness, *The Gravedigger File* (London: Hodder & Stoughton, 1983), pp. 42, 45.

17 Kathryn C. Montgomery, *Target: Prime Time: Advocacy Groups and the Struggle over Entertainment Television* (New York: Oxford University Press, 1989), pp. 78–79.

two other main vehicles of persuasion have been harnessed—the media and education.

Media Magic

One of the most successful TV series in recent years is *Sex and the City*, a programme about a group of chic single women, who, as the title suggests, engage in a fairly free and easy sexual lifestyle. The idea of cheating on your partner and not telling him about it has been taken up by another TV series, *Desperate Housewives*. Infidelity has become the order of the day in much mainstream entertainment. Lee Siegel has argued that it is not coincidental that the creators of both *Sex and the City* and *Desperate Housewives* are all gay men.[18] He suggests that what was going on was, 'an ingenious affirmation of a certain type of gay-male sexuality' which is notoriously promiscuous. This was brought to the fore by a ground-breaking survey in *The New York Times* in 2010 which revealed that about half of gay couples in San Francisco who were in a permanent relationship held to sexual openness, which, far from harming gay unions, is said to enrich them.[19] Referring to *Sex and the City*, Siegel called it, 'the biggest hoax perpetrated on straight single women in the history of entertainment'. Single women who see themselves portrayed in these relationships are actually watching a justification for the gay men who produce the show. Therefore the portrayal of women behaving this way

---

18 Cited by Charles Colson, *Lies that go Unchallenged in Popular Culture*, (Carol Stream: Tyndale House Publishers, 2005), pp. 306–307.

19 *The New York Times* (28th of January, 2010).

makes it easier to accept promiscuous homosexuality. In other words fiction is being used to perpetrate a fiction.

In 1996, the gay writer David Ehrenstein wrote an article in which he acknowledged '[t]here are openly gay writers on almost every major prime-time situation comedy you can think of.' He lists: *Friends, Seinfeld, Murphy Brown, Roseanne, Mad about You, The Nanny, Wings, The Single Guy, Caroline in the City, Coach, Dave's World, Home Court, High Society, The Crew,* and *Boston Common.* Ehrenstein concludes: 'In short, when it comes to sitcoms, gays rule.'[20]

Education, Education, Indoctrination

As the members of N.I.C.E. and the Frankfurt School recognised, capturing people's minds (and hearts) through education is central to any strategy for a lasting social revolution. As lesbian activist Patricia Warren notes, 'Whoever captures the kids, owns the future.'[21] Lukács, as we have seen, would have wholeheartedly agreed. After all, he tried to do it in his native Hungary!

This lies behind the Educate and Celebrate movement in the United Kingdom (which draws some of its funds from the BBC's Children in Need appeal). The web site reads:

> Educate & Celebrate is an Ofsted and DFE recognised Best Practice Award Programme that gives staff,

---

20 David Ehrenstein, "More than Friends," *Los Angeles Magazine* (May 1996).

21 Cited by Lisa Nolland, 'Children as Gay Champions?' http://www.e-n.org.uk/2015/10/features/children-as-gay-champions/9b70c/ [accessed: 20/12/2019]

students, parents and governors the confidence and strategies to implement an LGBT+Inclusive curriculum to successfully eradicate homophobia, biphobia and transphobia from our nursery, primary and secondary schools, colleges, Universities, organisations and communities [...] Our aim is to ensure that educational establishments and organisations adhere to their statutory duty of LGBT+Inclusion in an accessible, comprehensive and creative way by treating everyone equally and fairly according to the Equality Act 2010 [...] Our own surveys 2015 revealed that almost half our students across the country are not receiving any form of LGBT+Inclusive education with 53% of schools not teaching about LGBT+ relationships and 49% of schools not teaching the definitions of lesbian, gay, bisexual and trans+. In fact only 3% of schools said they had LGBT+ activity in 2 or more subject areas, which could explain why 76% of teachers said they'd had no LGBT+ specific training and 44% of schools contacted us initially because staff were not confident in dealing with sexual orientation or gender identity [...] Educate & Celebrate responds to these needs by engaging all stakeholders in the journey to inclusion to make our educational establishments, organisations and communities LGBT+Friendly.[22]

Elly Barnes of Educate and Celebrate is quite candid about the primary aim of the organisation which is 'to completely smash heteronormativity [...] that is what we

---

22 https://www.educateandcelebrate.org [accessed: 20/12/2019]

want to do so our kids can grow up to be who they are.'[23] This of course is wholly disingenuous for they don't want 'kids to grow up to be who they are' (which would be, on the whole, heterosexuals) but rather to mess them up in order to provide a greater pool from which homosexuals can fish, as well as promote, the myth of 'polymorphous perversity'.

Another example is the 'No Outsiders' teaching training resource by Andrew Moffat.[24] The use of this material in Birmingham's Parkfield Community School—Moffat's school which has a 98% Muslim intake—as well as five other schools in the area, resulted in the parents protesting outside the schools before withholding some of their children from attending. Not surprisingly the parents were labelled 'homophobic extremists' with the teachers being portrayed as victims who simply wanted to do their job. Moffat's own defence was that the 'No Outsiders' programme is simply 'designed to teach children that gays and lesbians exist'. That was the narrative being presented to the public. However, in his introduction, Moffat refers to his 2007 book *Challenging Homophobia in Primary School: An Early Years Resource*. In this earlier work, he said that his aim was to teach five-year-olds that gays and lesbians exist. However, he now believes that this is *unnecessary* because children—due to greater openness and the visibility of gay characters on television—already

---

23 https://anglicanmainstream.org/questioning-lgbt-education/ [accessed: 20/12/2019]

24 https://www.transgendertrend.com/no-outsiders-queering-primary-classroom/ [accessed: 20/12/2019]

know this. What we *now* need to teach children, he believes, is that:

> Homophobia once existed, but we don't have it in our schools today, and that to be a person who is gay or lesbian or transgender or bi-sexual is *normal, acceptable and ok*. Children also need to be learning that they may identify or may not identify as LGBT as they grow up, and that whoever they grow into as an adult is also perfectly normal and acceptable.[25]

That is also how Nick Gibb, the Minister for Schools, saw things according to his letter to the London Times,

> The protests outside a primary school in Birmingham which teaches the fact that same-sex relationships are normal and are as loving and supportive as any heterosexual relationship are in my view wrong. I support the city council's decision to secure an injunction against those protests taking place near the school. It is bizarre and horrific that we allow protesters outside primary schools with placards to target those who teach what is legal and wholly appropriate in today's society.[26]

In true Marxist style the rights of parents to decide what is appropriate for their children are overridden by the State, and the 'normalisation' of polymorphous sexuality

---

25 Moffat in: https://www.transgendertrend.com/no-outsiders-queering-primary-classroom/ [accessed: 01/01/2020].

26 Nick Gibb, 'It's wrong to protest about the teaching of gay relationships' (June 6th, 2019), https://www.thetimes.co.uk/article/it-s-wrong-to-protest-about-the-teaching-of-gay-relationships-t0g85vxx6 [accessed: 20/12/2019]

is being peddled in a way which would no doubt have
delighted Marcuse but horrified Freud.

Warwickshire County Council have a web site called
Respect Yourself designed to give advice on sexual
relationships for young teenagers, containing this 'value
free' assessment:

> Unfortunately, sex doesn't come with an instruction
> manual or map of the pitfalls and it certainly
> doesn't come with a moral compass. People see
> sex in many different lights and have sex for many
> different reasons.[27]

Parson Street Primary School in Bristol invited Drag
Queen Story Time to read books promoting alternative
lifestyles to their children. Drag Queen Story Time
founder Tom Canham said:

> We have an opportunity to provide our children with
> a better world in which to grow up, free from fear
> of rejection, or abuse, for being who they are—and
> Drag Queen Story Time is proud to be working with
> fantastic organisations all across the country to help
> make that a reality.[28]

Silencing the Lambs

We have already noted Marcuse's uncompromising
attitude to dissidents, that certain ideas are not to be

---

27 http://www.tell-someone.org/30281 [accessed: 01/01/2020]

28 http://www.breitbart.com/london/2018/02/25/backlash-drag-queens-primary-school
    [accessed: 26/12/2019]

expressed (and it is a short step from forbidding the expression of ideas to banning ideas). This is now working itself out aggressively in our various institutions.

In 2016 Felix Ngole had said during a Facebook debate that 'the Bible and God identify homosexuality as a sin.' On the basis of this he was removed from his two year MA course in Social work at Sheffield University. Writing in *The Sun,* columnist Rod Liddle commented:

> Frankly, I think our social services departments could do with rather more people who have strong, Christian principles instead of the inept, hand-wringing, liberal halfwits who allowed the vile abuse of children to go on across the country [...] But even that's not the main point. Universities are supposed to be places where a huge diversity of views can be heard. Not any more, not in our universities. If you don't subscribe to every one of their modern, secular, liberal beliefs you're out on your ear. Either banned from speaking at their campuses or thrown off your course. Just because you believe in something that they don't.[29]

In 2019 the Court of Appeal overturned a High Court decision to uphold Felix Ngole's expulsion from Sheffield University, thus giving a slight reprieve from the 'hideous strength' which is now casting its long dark shadow over many UK universities.

---

29 Cited in Julian Mann, *Christians in the Community of the Dome* (Welwyn Garden City: Evangelical Press, 2017), pp. 62–63.

Get Connected

We have spoken of <u>Babel-connectivity and N.I.C.E. using</u> <u>technology; both of these come together with today's</u> <u>social media.</u> <u>Whole causes can be orchestrated becoming</u> <u>worldwide news (fake or otherwise) within a matter of</u> <u>hours.</u> Furthermore, <u>Marcuse's call to silence those who</u> <u>would oppose the revolution has become much easier with</u> <u>a lynch mob mentality being able to be whipped up with</u> <u>ease via Facebook, Twitter and the like</u>. Understandably with such a possibility of this happening people will want to keep their heads down and mouths shut!

'This new "sexual" agenda is […] a remaking of human "identity"', writes Professor Peter Jones:

> We are dealing with a neo-Marxism so committed to a classless egalitarian society that it must eradicate by any means possible embodied gender distinctions, which are the final bulwark of creational difference, written into our DNA. <u>The goal is no longer a classless society</u> <u>but a classless mind and a genderless body—no longer</u> <u>just a fair deal for the worker but a transformation</u> <u>of the human psyche! At this point, such a powerful</u> <u>cosmology takes on an unmistakably religious</u> <u>character.</u>[30] *IT IS A RELIGION OF* *REPLACEMENT OF GOD WITH SELF.*

There are <u>two institutions which are seen to be barriers</u> *A RELIGION OF BABEL.*

---

30 Peter Jones, 'A Response to Rod Dreher's "Sex After Christianity"' 2014), http://www.reformation21.org/featured/a-response-to-rod-drehers-sex-after-christianity.php [accessed: 20/12/2019]

to achieving this agenda and both are intrinsically related: the family and the church, to which we now turn.

Chapter 5
Barbarians Through The Gates

WHILE APPEARING TO PORTRAY GAY MARRIAGE AND GAY families as simply variants along a sociological spectrum, the end game of the neo-Marxist agenda is the destruction of the family. According to the *Communist Manifesto*, 'the bourgeois family will vanish as a matter of course when its complement [private property] vanishes, and both will vanish with the vanishing of capital'.[1] One way Marx and Engels envisaged this being achieved was by replacing home education with social education. As we have seen in the previous chapter, those who are determined in forwarding the progressive agenda see schools as one of the primary battle grounds to be won. This circumvents the parent's traditional role in passing on values to the next generation thus capturing one of Gramsci's 'commanding heights' of a culture.

---

[1]   Karl Marx, "Critique of the Gotha Program (1875)" in *Karl Marx and Friedrich Engels: Selected Works*, Vol. 2 (Moscow: Progress Publishers, 1970), p. 22.

Unhappy Families

I have already considered the influence of Marcuse and the promotion of polymorphous perversity, but this required the abolition of the traditional patriarchal family:

> No longer used as a full-time instrument of labour, the body would be resexualized, (which) would first manifest itself in a reactivation of all erotogenic zones and, consequently, in a resurgence of pregenital polymorphous sexuality and in a decline of genital supremacy. The body in its entirety would become an object of cathexis, a thing to be enjoyed— an instrument of pleasure. <u>This change in the value and scope of libidinal relations would lead to a disintegration of the institutions in which the private interpersonal relations have been 'reorganized,' particularly the monogamic and patriarchal family.</u>[2]

i.e.: — DESTROYED

The intention is clear—destroy the family!

Others have been more explicit in their aim. For example, <u>the Gay Liberation Front Manifesto states</u>:

> <u>Equality is never going to be enough; what is needed is a total social revolution, a complete reordering of civilization</u>. <u>Reform [...] cannot change the deep-down attitude of straight people that homosexuality is at best inferior to their own way of life, at worst a sickening perversion. It will take more than reforms to change</u>

---

2 Cited in Breshears, 'The Origins of Cultural Marxism and Political Correctness', p. 53.

this attitude, because it is rooted in our society's most
basic institution the—Patriarchal Family.[3]

More recently, the Lesbian author and activist Masha
Gessen let the proverbial gay cat out of the neo-Marxist
bag when she said,

> Fighting for gay marriage generally involves lying about
> what we're going to do with marriage when we get
> there. Because we lie that the institution of marriage is
> not going to change, and that is a lie. The institution of
> marriage is going to change and it should change, and
> again, I don't think it should exist.[4]

It is therefore somewhat disturbing to find the
Archbishop of Canterbury, Justin Welby, acquiescing to
this redefining and slow destruction of the family. In a
lecture he delivered in Moscow in 2017, Welby said,

> The place where most people forge their first
> relationships is within the family. It is easy, however,
> *to define what makes up the family very narrowly* [...]
> The reality is that family life is and always has been
> complex. In the United Kingdom in the last forty
> years there has been a great shift in the understanding
> and the reality of family life [...] In recent years in a
> number of nations, including the United Kingdom,
> same-sex, or as it is called in law, equal marriage, is

---

3   *Gay Liberation Front: Manifesto* (London: Russell Press Ltd, 1971).

4   Cited by Gavin Ashenden, 'Sinister agenda to replace families with Big Brother',
    https://ashenden.org/2018/03/15/when-the-silly-becomes-the-sinister-the-latest-
    round-in-the-culture-wars/ [accessed: 20/12/2019]

now understood to be normal, acceptable and unchallengeable in many countries [...] The speed of change has led many constituencies such as churches and other faith groups to find themselves living in a culture that they have not even begun to come to terms with [...] The family, *however it is experienced*, is the place where we can be at our strongest and most secure [...] It is a gift of God in any society, bearing burdens, supporting the vulnerable and stabilising both those who believe themselves autonomous and those who feel themselves to be failures' (italics mine).[5]

It is obvious that the Archbishop wants to defend and strengthen the place of the family in society, but by implying that biblical norms regarding what constitutes family are too 'narrowly defined', Welby unthinkingly falls into line with the neo-Marxist drum beat that the family is a malleable concept which can (and should) be changed or even got rid of altogether, thus making himself a 'useful idiot'. — DISAGREE. HE'S A TRUE BELIEVER IN THE NEO-MARXIST STRATEGY. *[handwritten annotations: ?, NAH, HE KNOWS, WHAT HE'S DOING.]*

Will Jones, may be scathing in his criticism of the Archbishop, but his logic is unimpeachable when he writes:

If this is in fact the case, then from a traditional Christian point of view it is baffling, not to mention seriously endangering Christian moral living and integrity of witness to the revelation of God in

---

5   See, http://anglicanmainstream.org/the-c-of-es-same-sex-marriage-of-convenience/ [accessed: 20/12/2019]

Christ. For in what other area of life, other than this one of sex, gender and family, would it be thought appropriate to encourage the church merely to come to terms with contemporary realities, and not to evaluate them, challenge them, and point to a better way in closer conformity with the Creator's designs? There are many complex realities, alongside broken families and wounded childhoods, with which modern people live—drug addiction, alcohol abuse, the sexualisation of children, corruption, destitution, slavery—yet for how many of them would the church counsel, or even appear to counsel, Christians merely to accept them and come to terms with them with no further comment or analysis? The apparent surrender of the church to the world's ideas in this particular area of sex, marriage and family is deeply disturbing to observe—not unlike watching a car crash in slow motion.[6]

Traditionally the Church has been the bastion of the family and so capturing the Church is strategic if the revolution is to be completed and the 'hideous strength' is to hold sway. More so, if one of the more traditional denominations cracks, that will have a far greater impact on public perception.

Burning Down the House

The two church institutions which are primary targets for

---

6   https://www.conservativewoman.co.uk/will-jones-c-es-sex-marriage [accessed: 20/12/2019]

the sex revisionist agenda are the Roman Catholic Church and the Church of England.

The Roman Catholic Church has been perceived, by the public at least, to be traditional in its position on heterosexual marriage and the unacceptability of same-sex relations. That seems to be changing under Pope Francis. In 2015 he appointed Dominican Father Timothy Radcliffe as a consultor for the Pontifical Council for Justice and Peace. As a contributor to the 2013 Church of England Pilling Report on human sexual ethics, Father Radcliffe said of homosexuality:

> How does all of this bear on the question of gay sexuality? We cannot begin with the question of whether it is permitted or forbidden! We must ask what it means, and how far it is Eucharistic. Certainly it can be generous, vulnerable, tender, mutual and non-violent. So in many ways, I would think that it can be expressive of Christ's self-gift. We can also see how it can be expressive of mutual fidelity, a covenantal relationship in which two people bind themselves to each other for ever.[7] —— HERETIC.

We saw in the character of the Revd Straik in Lewis's novel how religious terminology was skilfully used as a Trojan horse to promote naturalistic materialism, something similar is now happening in the promotion of a new paganism.

Similarly religious language is used and abused to make

---

7   *The Pilling Report* (London: Church House, 2013), p. 77.

the Bible say the opposite of what it does say, thus scaling heaven to bring God down.

Old Heresies in New Guises

In July 2017, Jayne Ozanne (who claims to be evangelical) placed a private member's motion to the General Synod meeting in York (GS 2070A) calling upon the Synod to effectively repudiate the practice of conversion therapy for those who experience same-sex attraction.[8] Contained in her summary statement is a heresy which no one thought to challenge:

> The Bible teaches us that we are each fearfully and wonderfully made (Psalm 139:14), and that we should praise God's gift of our creation. Thus, our diversity as human beings is a reflection of God's creativity and something to celebrate. The biblical concern is not with what we are but how we choose to live our lives, meaning that differing sexual orientations and gender

---

8   Core Issues Trust points out that gay conversion therapy is a 'disparaging nickname given to a field of intrusive psychological and medical treatments aiming to alter a person's sexual desires. Such therapies, using drugs and electronic equipment, were largely discontinued 50 years ago.' However, 'Many different talking therapies are used to assist individuals who are troubled by patterns of thought and behaviour, which disrupts their quality of life. While society is now largely accepting of homosexual practice, some people are troubled by their experience of same-sex attraction, perhaps for reasons of religious faith, or wanting to maintain a faithful heterosexual marriage; others may be concerned about the health risks associated with a gay lifestyle. They therefore want to explore the possibility of reducing those feelings and moving away from those behaviours. There are methods of therapy and counselling which many have found helpful in achieving this result.' https://www.core-issues.org/news/what-is-conversion-therapy [accessed: 20/12/2019]

identities are not inherently sinful, nor mental health disorders to be "cured".

The partial truth, which is taken and exaggerated and presented as the whole truth, appears in the first sentence of her quotation. This has been taken by Christians in the past as a basis for the sanctity of human life which is undermined by the practice of abortion.[9] However, it is a *non sequitur* for Ozanne to then conclude 'Thus, our diversity as human beings is a reflection of God's creativity and something to celebrate.' If anything, as we have noted, it is the belief in human sanctity which is to be protected which logically arises out of this passage, not human diversity. This is followed up by falsehood for it is certainly *not* the case that the Bible isn't concerned with 'what we are' but simply 'how we choose to live our lives.' How we choose and what we choose at least in part arises from 'what we are' in terms of our dispositions. Some of those dispositions are towards things which God forbids (such as idolatry, greed and same-sex relations) and not only flow from 'what we are' (idolaters, gluttons, homosexuals, etc.) but reinforces what we are becoming.

The missing doctrine which is necessary to check the heresy Ozanne and her supporters like the Bishop of Liverpool, Paul Bayes, are promoting is the doctrine of original sin. To be sure, according to the Psalmist we are 'fearfully and wonderfully made', but according to the same psalmist in Psalm 51:5, 'I was sinful at birth, sinful

---

9   For example, Nigel M. de S. Cameron and Pamela F. Sims, *Abortion: the crisis in Morals and Medicine* (Illinois: Inter Varsity Press, 1986), p. 22.

from the time my mother conceived me.' At both one and the same time, David is 'fearfully and wonderfully made' in the womb and 'sinful' from the moment he was conceived. We are, as Immanuel Kant once said, 'warped wood', or, again, as Luther put it, *'incurvartus in se'* or even, to use traditional terminology, contaminated by original sin which, according to Article 9 of the 39 articles of the Church of England, is 'the fault and corruption of the Nature of everyman […] and is of his own nature inclined to evil.'

Jayne Ozanne is effectively promoting two heresies at once.

The first is Pelagianism.

In the fifth century, the monk Pelagius argued that 'Evil is not born with us, and we are procreated without fault; and the only thing in men at their birth is what God has formed.' This was effectively dealt with by St. Augustine and condemned decisively at the Council of Carthage in 418 with the condemnation being ratified at the Council of Ephesus in 431.[10]

The second heresy, called Socinianism, is a variation of the first and is named after its exponent, Faustus Socinus (the Latinised name for Fausto Sozzini 1539–1604). This teaching has been effectively summarized by Andrew Fuller,

---

10 See Mathew Roberts, 'Why Pelagianism Matters (including for the Church of England)': https://matthewpwroberts.wordpress.com/2017/07/18/why-pelagianism-matters-including-to-the-church-of-england/ [accessed: 20/12/2019]

> They consider all evil propensities in men (except those which are accidently contracted by education or example) as being, in every sense, natural to them; supposing that they were originally created with them; they cannot, therefore be offensive to God, unless he could be offended with the work of his own hands for being what he made it.[11]

But this is to engage with issues in terms of reason and argument which is shunned by cultural Marxism as tactically dangerous. Far better to throw in a few positive phrases such as being 'fearfully and wonderfully made' so that those who are seen to be questioning the proponent appear to be the heretical ones.

The way in which cultural Marxism has triumphed in the General Synod of the Church of England as reflected in the Ozanne debate has been well articulated by the General Synod member, Dr Chik Kaw Tan.[12] He observes that at Synod, 'Theology is seen to get in the way of real life. The little theological context there is focuses on love, acceptance, equality and justice', the very stuff of Marcuse. He further reflects:

> 12 years ago when I first joined Synod, the LGBT lobby consisted of a little stand with a few people handing out leaflets. Many Synod members subtly changed the direction of movement away from them

---

11 A.G. Fuller, *The Complete Works of the Rev. Andrew Fuller* (Philadelphia: American Baptist Publication Society, 1856), p. 54.

12 Chik Kaw Tan, 'Fundamental shifts in the General Synod', https://www.gafcon.org/news/fundamental-shifts-in-the-general-synod [accessed: 20/12/2019]

and politely avoided any conversation with LGBT activists. 12 years on, they are the all-winning victorious juggernaut, crushing all in its path. Not only is the LGBT constituency well and truly embedded in the organisational structure of the Church of England, its agenda for change dominates proceedings.

The LGBT long march has almost arrived at its final destination in the Church of England.

"No sanctity in sex please—we're religious"

Sometimes non-Christians on the outside seem to be more insightful about the church than Christians who are on the inside. Camille Paglia is one such person.[13]

In her essay, 'The Joy of Presbyterian Sex', she exposes the neo-Marxist gullibility which is a feature of much liberal Christianity.[14] Writing about the Presbyterian Church's report on Human sexuality (USA), she comments,

> The committee's prescription for an enlightened Christianity is "learning from the marginalized." This new liberal cliché is repeated so often that I began to misread it as "margarinized." We are told that "those of us with varying degrees of social power and status must now move away from the center, so that other, more marginalized voices [...] may be heard." But the report picks and chooses its marginalized outcasts as

---

13 Camille Paglia, *Sex, Art and American Culture* (New York: Vintage Books, 1992).
14 Paglia, *Sex, Art and American Culture*, pp. 226–237.

snobbishly as Proust's Duchesse de Guermantes. We can move tender, safe, clean, hand-holding gays and lesbians to the center—but not, of course, pederasts, prostitutes, strippers, pornographers, or sadomasochists. And if we're going to learn from the marginalized, what about drug dealers, moonshiners, Elvis impersonators, string collectors, Mafiosi, foot fetishists, serial murderers, cannibals, Satanists, and the Ku Klux Klan? I'm sure they'll all have a lot to say. The committee gets real prudish real fast when it has to deal with sexuality outside its feminist frame of reference: "Incest is abhorrent and abhorred," it flatly declares. I wrote in the margin, "No lobbyists, I guess!"[15]

Carl Trueman in pondering Paglia's remarks asks, 'So why do Christians capitulate to such nonsense so easily?' He answers,

Here Paglia and I are on the same page: Because the Christian church is too often not satisfied with being the Christian church, with all of its austere dogma and demands, but prefers to be merely an insipid and derivative mouthpiece for modern emotivism. Liberal churches do what they always do: In an effort to remain credible they dutifully turn up to baptize whatever sentimental mush the world wants to promote on the trendy topic of the moment. Of course, it always does this a day or two late, but that's what happens when your ethics are simply a response to norms which the world has already embraced. No longer is it 'Thus saith

15 Paglia, *Sex, Art and American Culture* , *p. 31.*

the Lord!' so much as 'Now, now, poor dear, you just do what feels right for you. Oh, and please, whatever you do, don't feel guilty about it.'[16]

The church increasingly adds its own confused voice to the confusing voices of the Babel culture in which it finds itself. <u>Marcuse's goal to 'destabilise language' is being helped along by the double speak of the church</u>.

Blurring the Boundaries

The exchange of a biblical cosmology for a new pagan one is also much in evidence in the Church of England as shown by the recent debates on gender.

Following the affirmation of transgender people in the July 2017 General Synod and the House of Bishops' permission to clergy to adapt liturgy to indicate acknowledgement of gender change, the trajectory is clear as are the underlying views regarding sexuality. <u>It is now expected that churches simply accept that a 'trans person' is not just identifying a gender different from his/her biological sex, but that he/she is ontologically different</u>. <u>This is a new narrative. No longer is a transgender person someone who feels trapped in the wrong body, this is a new variant of what it means to be human</u>. The boundaries of creation have not simply been set aside, they have been wiped away.

---

16 'The Joy of Paglian Sex', Posted on Monday, September 18, 2017 by Carl Trueman on Postcards from Palookavil- http://www.alliancenet.org/mos/postcards-from-palookaville/the-joy-of-paglian-sex [accessed: 20/12/2019]

Someone who has taken the removal of boundaries and distinctions to a whole new level is Judith Butler; she is not a neo-Marxist but a poststructuralist. For Butler identity is free-flowing and flexible, not fixed. There is no masculine or feminine being, only performance behaviours which can change with time. She is the champion of Queer theory—a term to refer to anything which is not heterosexual; the opposing of homosexuality with heterosexuality should be eliminated in favour of the complete dissolution of sexual identity for only then will the 'hegemony of compulsory heterosexuality' be completely overcome and people will be free to invent themselves.[17]

All of this is fully in-line with the liberation desired by the cultural Marxists; if sexual identity is a social construct like everything else, then use technology to bring nature into line. But this is completely contrary to the biblical vision which is ably described by Professor Oliver O'Donovan,

> One can express the Christian perspective like this: the either-or of biological maleness and femaleness to which the human race is bound is not a meaningless or oppressive condition of nature; it is the good gift of God, because it gives rise to possibilities of relationship in which the polarities of masculine and feminine, more

---

17 See Gabriele Kuby, *The Global Sexual Revolution: the destruction of freedom in the name of freedom* (LifeSite: 2015), pp.44–48.

subtly nuanced than the biological differentiation, can play a decisive part.[18]

Culture Clash

Here the clash of cosmologies symbolised by the Tower of Babel is brought into sharp focus. Either there is objective reality to which we are to conform our minds, senses, and values and so have genuine human flourishing within the boundaries God has given, or all such claims are to be regarded with suspicion and further expressions of 'repressive tolerance.' Os Guinness remarks:

> The story of creation is a story of distinctions, a story of discrimination between heaven and earth, which the Tower of Babel tries to undo, between male and female, etc. In fact, the Jews called the Lord, "the Great Discriminator," because His creation discriminates between things, and if you remove the discriminations, you create idols; they're much closer in their understanding of the deadliness of some of the ideas at the heart of the sexual revolution.[19]

When God removes the boundaries in judgement, creation collapses in on itself in chaos as at the Flood; when we begin to remove the boundaries, society collapses in on itself in excessive self-confidence.

---

18 Oliver O' Donovan, *Transsexualism and Christian Marriage* (Grove Booklet on Ethics, No. 46:1982), p. 7.

19 Os Guinness, *Christian Courage and the Struggle for Civilization*, (C.S. Lewis Institute, Volume 2, Number 4:2017) p. 6.

Although it is a distasteful subject, <u>the next blurring of the boundaries is not between human sexes, but human and non-human—zoophilia. Here we see the full corruption of human hubris</u>. Journalist, Malcolm J. Brenner, achieved notoriety by having sex with a dolphin; the subject of his award-winning documentary *Dolphin Lover*.[20] He describes himself as a zoophile. He believes his zoophilia is the result of the 'very intense physical and sexual abuse' he claims to have suffered in early childhood at the hands of psychologist Albert Duvall, a student of the controversial psychoanalyst Wilhelm Reich of the Frankfurt School. 'I think I found animals to be a safe and secure repository for my sexual desires,' he says in the documentary. Brenner draws parallels between current anti-bestiality laws and the anti-miscegenation laws of the nineteenth and twentieth centuries in the USA because, as he says in the documentary, '150 years ago, black people were considered a degenerate sub-species of the human being [...] And I'm hoping that in a more enlightened future, zoophilia will be no more regarded as controversial or harmful than interracial sex is today.'

Others, like Cody Beck, draw a different parallel; being a zoophile in modern American society, Beck says, is 'like being gay in the 1950s. You feel like you have to hide, that if you say it out loud, people will look at you like a freak.'[21] <u>It is difficult to argue against this if the neo-Marxist thesis is correct regarding social constructionism.</u>

---

20 https://www.youtube.com/watch?v=aEX33vAyF5Y [accessed: 20/12/2019]

21 http://www.miaminewtimes.com/news/animal-instincts-6378144#Comments [accessed: 20/12/2019]

But people do argue against it on moral grounds. For example, Piers Beirne, author of *Confronting Animal Abuse,* says that because there is an imbalance of power involved, the animals which are sexually engaged in this way are invariably domestic 'completely dependent upon us for food, water, shelter and affection'. He concludes, 'I think it is morally wrong for a human to have sex with non-human animals for exactly the same reason it's wrong for him to have sex with human babies or adolescents.'[22] But what is the moral basis for arguing that it is the imbalance of power which is the morally deciding factor? Why should this be regarded as morally wrong? If one were to adopt a consequentialist approach to ethics, that such activity could be shown to be harmful to those involved and wider society in the long run, then that might have some traction. But of course if one were to go down this line then one would have to apply the same reasoning to homosexual behaviour and promiscuity, which people are loathed to do. We are back to a neo-Marxist concern that abuse of power is the only thing that is forbidden.[23]

---

22 *Ibid.*

23 The arts have also got into the act, quite literally as we see in Edward Albee's 'Goat or Who is Sylvia? ' which has recently been performed in London with actor Damien Lewis in the lead. It is a tale of a married, middle-aged architect, Martin, his wife Stevie, and their son Billy, whose lives crumble when Martin falls in love with a goat. The play focuses on the limits of an ostensibly liberal society. Through showing this family in crisis, Albee challenges audience members to question their own moral judgment of social taboos.

The Abolition of God and the Abolition of Man

The end result of all poststructuralist philosophies of the like of Foucault and Derrida is not the liberation of human beings but their destruction—'the abolition of man.' Let us not be under any illusions as to what is at stake. Hannah Arendt showed in her reporting of the trial of Hitler's chief architect of the Final Solution, Adolf Eichmann, that he and those like him were only able to carry out their atrocities by separating themselves from their victims by denying the common humanity which connected them both.[24] In the words of Carl Trueman in his essay 'The Banality of Evil', 'The possibility of the Final Solution was predicated on the abolition of common human nature.'[25] If there is no common human nature, it is difficult to see what basis there is for human rights. Why should this too be any less of a social construct, one which can be made and unmade by the dominant social class of the time? Indeed, for the cultural Marxist such rights need to be formulated and given legislative force to impose the new liberty.[26] If it is a human right for those who are gay

---

24 Hannah Arendt, *Eichmann in Jerusalem: A Report on the Banality of Evil* (London: Penguin, 1977).

25 Carl Trueman, 'The Banality of Evil', in *Minority Report* (Mentor: Christian Focus Publications, 2008), p. 82.

26 'Surely, no government can be expected to foster its own subversion, but in a democracy such a right is vested in the people (i.e. in the majority of the people). This means that the ways should not be blocked on which a subversive majority could develop, and if they are blocked by organized repression and indoctrination, their reopening may require apparently undemocratic means. They would include the withdrawal of toleration of speech and assembly from groups and movements which promote aggressive policies, armament, chauvinism, discrimination on the grounds of race and religion, or which oppose the extension of public services, social

to marry, it will be unacceptable to have a society which refuses it. It will be forbidden to forbid.

The Issue is Never the Issue

Saul Alinsky was one of the most influential radical organisers in the United States in the twentieth century and was mentor to both Barack Obama and Hillary Clinton. David Horowitz relates how Alinsky used to welcome newcomers who volunteered to become community organisers. He first asked them why they volunteered in the first place. Many would respond with idealistic claims of wanting to help the poor and oppressed. Alinsky would then scream at them like a Marine Corps drill instructor, 'No! You want to organise for power!'[27]

Without wishing to suggest that there is no concern by members of the progressive Left for those perceived to be poor and marginalised, neither should we lose sight of the overruling principle that the 'means justifies the end' in such an ideology. As a writer in the 1960's radical Students for a Democratic Society publication, *New Left Notes* ably put it, 'The issue is never the issue. The issue is always the revolution.'[28]

---

security, medical care, etc. Moreover, the restoration of freedom of thought may necessitate new and rigid restrictions on teachings and practices in the educational institutions which, by their very methods and concepts, serve to enclose the mind within the established universe of discourse and behaviour.' Marcuse, *op cit.*, p. 88.

27 Horowitz, *The Dark Agenda*, p. 84.
28 Horowitz, *The Dark Agenda*, p. 84.

Greengrocers and Lanyards

If Carl Trueman and others are correct in their analysis that in a very meaningful sense we are now all in 'Marx's world' and heirs to a revolution brought about by cultural Marxism, then we might be helped to understand the nature of that dominant social imaginary and how we might work towards its change by listening to someone who, for many years, lived under such a system. One person who has much to teach us is the late Vacláv Havel.

Havel was one of the leading members of the Charter 77 Movement which led to the 'Velvet Revolution' in Czechoslovakia in 1989. Their motto was 'Live the Truth.' Eleven years earlier, in 1978, Havel wrote a deeply insightful essay, 'The Power of the Powerless.'[29] In it he described the communist system which held most of Eastern Europe in its iron grip as a 'post-totalitarian system' to distinguish it from traditional dictatorships. This was a 'dictatorship of a political bureaucracy over a society which has undergone economic and social levelling.'[30] The bureaucracy enforces and maintains an ideology, in this case Marxism, which is attractive to the citizens in that it provides some sort of cohesion to life, giving the individual an identity derived from the system. There is, however, a high price tag attached, namely, the 'abdication of one's own reason, conscience, and responsibility, for an essential aspect of this ideology

---

29 See Vacláv Havel, 'The Power of the Powerless' https://s3.amazonaws.com/Random_Public_Files/powerless.pdf [accessed: 01/01/2020]

30 'The Power of the Powerless', p. 2.

is the consignment of reason and conscience to a higher authority.'[31]

How does such a post-totalitarian society acquire well-meaning citizens, who, if asked and allowed to express themselves freely, would not countenance such an ideology and society for a moment, to conform and, more than that, collude with 'the system'?[32]

To answer that question, Havel employs a homely illustration. He asks us to imagine a scene where a greengrocer places a sign in his shop window amongst the carrots and onions. The sign reads: 'Workers of the world unite!' Havel then asks: What is the greengrocer trying to communicate by doing such a thing? Is it that he is personally enthusiastic about the idea and, therefore, this action expresses his socialistic fervour? Havel suggests not. He does it, maintains Havel, because he has been asked to do it and has been doing it for years as have countless other shopkeepers—everyone does it. And that is the point—*everyone* does it. The slogan, argues Havel, is a sign containing:

A subliminal but definite message: Verbally, it might

---

31 'The Power of the Powerless', p. 4.

32 Havel explains what he means by 'the system': 'What we understand by the system is not, therefore, a social order imposed by one group upon another, but rather something which may seem impossible to grasp or define (for it is in the nature of a mere principle), but which is expressed by the entire society as an important feature of its life.' 'The Power of the Powerless', p. 17. With this understanding we can confidently say there is a 'system' operating in the UK and many other secularised countries which according to our thesis is an expression of a more insidious system by the 'rulers and principalities' of an invisible order.

be expressed this way: "I, the greengrocer XY, live here and I know what I must do. I behave in the manner expected of me. I can be depended upon and am beyond reproach. I am obedient and therefore I have the right to be left in peace." This message, of course, has an addressee: it is directed above, to the greengrocer's superior, and at the same time it is a shield that protects the greengrocer from potential informers.[33]

Havel points out that if the grocer were given a sign stating this unambiguously, he might even put up such a sign, but would be ashamed to do it:

To overcome this complication, his expression of loyalty must take the form of a sign which, at least on its textual surface, indicates a level of disinterested conviction. It must allow the greengrocer to say, "What's wrong with the workers of the world uniting?" Thus the sign helps the greengrocer to conceal from himself the low foundations of his obedience, at the same time concealing the low foundations of power. It hides them behind the facade of something high. And that something is ideology.[34]

An ideology, according to Havel, is 'a specious way of relating to the world. It offers human beings the illusion

33 'The Power of the Powerless', p. 6.
34 'The Power of the Powerless', p. 7.

of an identity, of dignity, and of morality while making it easier for them to part with them.'[35]

The point of the grocer displaying the sign in the window is not that it has to be taken literally, but the *subtext* is certainly meant to be taken seriously—for the display of such signs are 'givens' of the rules of the game. Displays of loyalty are expected, and any form of dissent—such as an unwillingness to display such signs—will not be tolerated. Not just by the higher powers, but by the other shopkeepers and workers like himself. They may not be any more devoted as Marxists than he is, but by failing to engage in displays of loyalty like this one, they endanger throwing the accepted social order into disarray. This may sound rather dramatic, but as Havel points out such public and highly visible symbols of loyalty and conformity are 'part of the panorama of everyday life.'[36] The details of the particular sign can be ignored, but its *significance* lies in the fact that it contributes to the panorama of signs and symbols and the 'PC language' which is all around.

> This panorama, of course, has a subliminal meaning as well: it reminds people where they are living and what is expected of them. It tells them what everyone else is doing, and indicates to them what they must do as well, if they don't want to be excluded, to fall into isolation,

---

35 'The primary excusatory function of ideology, therefore, is to provide people, both as victims and pillars of the post-totalitarian system, with the illusion that the system is in harmony with the human order and the order of the universe.' 'The Power of the Powerless', p. 7.

36 'The Power of the Powerless', p. 14.

alienate themselves from society, break the rules of the game, and risk the loss of their peace and tranquillity and security.[37]

Remember, <u>Havel is describing communist Czechoslovakia. But a moment's reflection soon reveals that, with a few minor changes of detail, he could be describing much of Western Europe and North America where its citizens are expected—on pain of social ostracization, loss of job, or even imprisonment— to display a similar loyalty to the cultural Marxism of our day</u>.

Signs in shop windows declaring 'Workers of the world unite' may not be required in the UK, but signs celebrating Gay pride month most certainly are. Let a manager of a local Sainsbury's store refuse to display such a sign and see what happens. Police stations, universities, town halls, and even cathedrals are expected to fly the rainbow flag and woe betide any transgressor who desists. National Trust employees, and, in some cases, teachers, are expected to wear rainbow lanyards that month and dissenters are made to feel uncomfortable at the very least. <u>Like Havel's greengrocer, very few of those who kowtow to the PC requirements of post-totalitarian Britain may actually have any firm convictions about so called 'gay rights', but they know what is expected of them and they also know what to expect if they don't conform</u>.[38]

---

37 'The Power of the Powerless', p. 14.

38 Havel describes the use of such instruments to get people to conform to the prevailing ideology as the principle of 'socio-totality.' He writes, 'Part of the essence

Hopefully by now it is clear that, as was the case with the Studdocks in Lewis's novel, countless 'pitiful souls' in the West, many of them children, have become the 'apocalyptic battleground of heaven'.

How should the church respond?

---

of the post-totalitarian system is that it draws everyone into its sphere of power, not so they may realize themselves as human beings, but so they may surrender their human identity in favour of the identity of the system, that is, so they may become agents of the system's general automatism and servants of its self-determined goals, so they may participate in the common responsibility for it, so they may be pulled into and ensnared by it, like Faust by Mephistopheles. More than this: *so they may create through their involvement a general norm and, thus, bring pressure to bear on their fellow citizens.* And further: *so they may learn to be comfortable with their involvement, to identify with it as though it were something natural and inevitable and, ultimately, so they may—with no external urging—come to treat any non-involvement as an abnormality, as arrogance, as an attack on themselves, as a form of dropping out of society.*' (Emphasis mine) 'The Power of the Powerless', pp. 15–16.

Chapter 6
Bringing Down Babel

THE PICTURE WHICH HAS BEEN PAINTED SEEMS RATHER bleak. But the church has had to face similar situations before. The Babel story repeats itself again and again throughout world history. In the words of G.K. Chesterton, 'At least five times [...] the Faith has to all appearances gone to the dogs. In each of these five cases, it was the dog that died.'[1]

In the aftermath of ruins of the Second World War, theologian Emile Brunner wrote:

> Sometimes I even think it is already too late. At any rate, if by the mercy of God we are to have some further breathing space, if He does grant us another chance to build up a new European civilization on the ruins of the old, facing all the time the possibility of an imminent

---

[1] G.K. Chesterton, *The Everlasting Man* (Nashville: Sam Torode Book Arts, 2017 [1925]), p. 201.

end to all civilized life on this globe, Christianity has a tremendous responsibility.[2]

That responsibility has not diminished in the twenty-first century.

Our hope as Christian believers against that 'hideous strength' is to be found within the account of the Tower of Babel itself.

Let me explain.

The story is presented in a chiastic structure which depicts a reversal of humankind's plans with the centre point being Genesis 11:5:

A 'the whole world had one language' (v. 1)
   B 'there' (v. 2)
      C 'each other' (v. 3)
         D 'Come, let's make bricks' (v. 3)
            E 'Come, let us build ourselves' (v. 4)
               F 'a city, with a tower' (v. 4)
                  G *the LORD came down* (v. 5)
               F[I] 'the city and the tower' (v. 5)
            E[I] 'that men were building' (v. 5)
         D[I] 'Come, let us […] confuse' (v. 7)
      C[I] 'each other' (v. 7)
   B[I] 'from there' (v. 8)
A[I] 'the language of the whole world' (v. 9)

Not only is the 'reversal' construction clearly visible, but

---

2 Emile Brunner, *Christianity and Civilization,* Vol 1: Foundations (London: Nisbet & Co., 1948), p. v.

it also paints a picture. When this diagram is turned on its side, the narrative of the Tower of Babel forms a picture of the Tower of Babel:

> YHWH's deliberation
> YHWH comes down–let us come down
> tower's top in heaven–on surface of the earth
> name for ourselves ————— name called Babel
> lest we be scattered ————— YHWH scattered them
> let us build a city ————— they stopped building the city
> settlement in Shinar ————— YHWH scattered them
> one language for all ————— YHWH confuses their languages
> all the earth————— over the face of all the earth [3]

In both representations it is *Yahweh's* action, not humankind's, which is final and decisive. Despite humankind's attempt to redefine and reconfigure reality— to 'de-god God'—it is God in his glorious omnipotence and infinite wisdom who remains Lord. He subverts all our attempts to subvert, and his great reality, which lies behind all realities, will win out.

While people use various means and idolatries to try and 'bring God down', it is God who elects to comes down and take captive all the rulers and authorities and principalities and powers. What verse 5 embodies is a principle which lies at the heart of the Bible, namely, that *God comes down in both judgement and mercy.* This was the

---

3   La Cocque cited in James Austin, *The Tower of Babel in Genesis: How the Tower of Babel Narrative Influences the Theology of Genesis and the Bible.*

basis for the hope of the Hebrew slaves in Exodus 3:8, 'I have come down'. Scott Oliphint comments:

> These four words could easily serve to frame the core of our understanding of God from Genesis to Revelation. There is no way to understand both who God is and his dealings with his creation without seeing it through this principle running throughout Scripture.[4]

It is this principle which finds its climax in the incarnation of the Eternal Logos, whose light still shines and is not mastered by darkness (John 1:5).

Christians have to carefully navigate between the Scylla of dewy-eyed optimism and the Charybdis of faithless pessimism. On the one hand the hold of modernity on the church can foster a can-do mentality which mimics that of the builders of the Tower of Babel—where employing the latest market techniques and following church growth indicators produces mega churches (although they may be little more than Christianised versions of the culture to which they are held captive).[5] On the other hand, a high sounding pietism marks a cultural retreat as, secure in their own subculture, evangelicals, in particular, remain doctrinally sound but become culturally irrelevant and their voice is not heard. Os Guinness strikes the right

---

4   K. Scott Oliphint, 'The Most Moved Mediator', *Themelios*, 30:1 (2004), 39–51 (p. 43).

5   David Wells has charted the way the evangelical church has adopted the marketing techniques of the surrounding culture with the call to go back to *sola Scriptura* rather than *sola cultura*. See David F. Wells, *The Courage to be Protestant: Truth-Lovers, Marketers, and Emergents in the Postmodern World* (Grand Rapids: Eerdmans, 2008).

biblical note which lies at the centre of the Babel episode emphasising *God's* action:

> Let it be clearly understood that our hope in the possibility of renewal is squarely grounded, not in ourselves, not in history and the fact that it has happened before, but in the power of God demonstrated by the truth of the resurrection of Jesus [...] This is therefore no time to hang our heads or hide our lights under any bushel for fear that we may be picked on for our refusal to fit in. We are to have no fear. We are to look up. We are to take strength from the fact that we can, because He can.[6]

Get Real!

Three things are necessary if, like Ransom and his small band of believers in Lewis's story, we are to challenge that 'hideous strength' in its present cultural Marxist form, namely, commending God's Truth, cultural engagement and courageous refusal and refutation.[7]

Commending God's Truth

If metaphysics is the study of 'what is', (which postmodernists would seek to deny), theology is the presentation of 'what is in Christ' (which radical

---

Os Guinness, *Renaissance: The Power of the Gospel However Dark the Times* (Illinois: Inter Varsity Press, 2014), pp. 144–145.

7   I have added the first to the other three elements proposed by Guinness in *Renaissance*, p. 85.

theological liberalism seeks to undermine).[8] The church of Christ should be in the business of presenting reality which comes from 'above' rather than trying to attempt with the world to reconstruct reality from 'below' with Babel hubris.

Three things are to be to the fore of the church's reality check.

First, the church must hold on to and hold out the reality of God in Christ, that is, his true *deity*—'the Word made flesh'. This is not a malleable God we can make in our own image. One that conforms to our idolatrous ideas and desires, or one that is domesticated and brought down according to our whim. He is the Creator who by a word stills the storm (Mark 4:35–41) and stops the forces of chaos (Mark 5:1–20). He comes to us as Judge who will not tolerate the established religious leaders who, by their man-made traditions, nullify the Word of God (Mark 7:1–23), and who would cause his little ones to stumble (Mark 9:42–50). He comes as Saviour to do that which we cannot do, reconcile us to God by his atoning sacrifice on the cross (Mark 10:45). As Vanhoozer writes in *The Pastor as Public Theologian*, 'Everything Jesus says, does and is reveals God. What there is in Christ is true knowledge of God.'[9]

In the second place what is in Christ is true *humanity*. This man Jesus (yes, biologically male with X and Y

8   Vanhoozer, *The Pastor as Public Theologian*, p. 110.

9   Vanhoozer, *The Pastor as Public Theologian*, p. 110.

chromosomes having a real human nature, which he still has in heaven seated at God's right hand) is the Son of Man, the Second (or last) Adam, showing us what it means to live the other-person centred life in delightful obedience to his Father. The model of Christ runs counter to the cultural Marxism in which human nature disappears together with human rights. Human nature, which the Second person of the Trinity assumed, is divinely given, not humanly fabricated. The undermining of the one will invariably lead to an undermining of the other.

The Battle for the Christ

It is not insignificant that the main battles in the early church against heresy centred on the blurring of the boundaries regarding the person and nature of Jesus Christ, a hideous attempt to refashion Reality if ever there was. There was the heresy of Arianism in the fourth century which denied the *deity* of Christ, viewing him as some kind of 'super-creature' who was *like* God the Father (Greek: *homoiousios*), but not of the *same* substance as the Father (Greek: *homoousios*). This was roundly condemned by the Council of Nicaea in 325.

Gnosticism on the other hand, denied the *humanity* of Christ; he only *seemed* to be human. Eutychianism in the fifth century postulated Christ as a 'hybrid', a chimera of deity and humanity, neither fully human nor fully divine but a third type of being, a man/god. The church, however, wished to do full justice to the boundaries

God had established in this unique self-revelation, as formulated in Chalcedon in 451, insisted that Jesus Christ was in nature *fully* human and *fully* divine, not confused or mixed, but two natures in one person. All heresies try to bring God down in true Babel fashion, but God chooses to come down in the way that he has decreed.

We should not therefore be surprised that as there is a confusing of boundaries in the present gender debates within the church today, there is also a confusing of the person and nature of the Lord Jesus Christ. Such distinctions as 'divinity', 'humanity' and 'sonship' suggest hierarchy and difference which the neo-Marxist cannot tolerate. And so we have this in a creed from the early 1990s declared at a World Council of Churches conference, 'I believe in God, MOTHER-FATHER-SPIRIT who called the world into being, who created men and women and set them free to live in love, in obedience and community.'[10] The publisher, LBI Institute, released a Bible entitled: *Judith Christ of Nazareth, The Gospels of the Bible, Corrected to Reflect that Christ Was a Woman, Extracted from Matthew, Mark, Luke and John.* These are further examples of 'breaking the established universe of meaning' central to the cultural Marxist strategy.

Third, what is in Christ is the whole created order, made by him, sustained by him, having its goal in him: 'All things were created through him and for him [...] and in him all things hold together' (Colossians 1:16–17).

---

10 See, 'Is God female?' in Melvin Tinker, *Touchy Topics* (Welwyn Garden City: Evangelical Press, 2016).

It is an 'order' and 'created' thus having a design and purpose; boundaries and spaces, which are determined by the Creator, not the creatures. In the Lord Jesus Christ, creation has a *telos*, a goal and end-point, and so contrary to the assertions of the postmodernists, there is an overarching story, a metanarrative. As Vanhoozer writes in 'Sapientail Apologetics', 'To think theologically is to understand persons, events and things (the parts) in relation to what is in Christ (the whole).[11]

These are some of the central immutable 'non-negotiables'[12] of the faith 'delivered once and for all to the saints' and the task of the church is to think and act theologically in understanding God, the world and ourselves in relation to Christ.[13] However, getting to grips with theology is only one half of the task, the other half is to understand our culture in order to be effective agents of change for Christ in the culture. It is a truism that 'those who are unaware of culture are doomed to repeat it.'

Cultural Engagement

The Church is easily drawn towards one of two extremes.

At one pole is what Peter Berger calls *cognitive and*

---

[11] Keven J. Vanhoozer, 'Sapiential Apologetics', in *Pictures at a Theological Exhibition* (Illinois: Inter Varsity Press, 2016), p. 235.

[12] This is a phrase owed to D.A. Carson in another context which conveys the idea that there are certain unchangeable beliefs which are not open to negotiation and so alteration, 'Factors Determining Current Hermeneutical Debate' in *Biblical Interpretation and the Church—Text and Context* ed. by D.A. Carson (Milton Keynes: Paternoster, 1984), p. 13.

[13] Carson, Biblical Interpretation and the Church, p. 111.

cultural resistance. Here the biblical call to flee the idols of the world in 1 Thessalonians 1:9 leads to a cultural isolation from the world as Christians form their own sub-culture which may owe more to fear than faithfulness. Such churches keep the world at a distance while making the occasional foray in evangelism.

Parallels have been drawn with the situation of the Church in pre-war Nazi Germany. In her article 'While The Church Sleeps', Lisa Nolland makes the astute observation that:

> We look back on the 1930s with angry incredulity at the blindness of German Christian leaders. How could they have ignored events at the heart of public life, occurring before their very eyes? Well, are we any different? The press of preaching duties, conferences, programmes, financial and pastoral crises, etc., mean that politically-incorrect, controversial issues just get buried. The herd/tribe mentality is as strong as that of 'Let's just be positive. God is good, all the time!' The culture in church circles is a million miles away from that of many secular workplaces. Moreover there are potent but subconscious assumptions made by leaders. Given (almost daily) LGBT conditioning, many in their flock now 'see the light', but because of the subconscious but tacit 'don't ask, don't tell', aren't saying.[14]

At the other extreme is *cognitive and cultural adaptation*

---

14 Lisa Nolland, 'While the Church Sleeps ...', https://www.e-n.org.uk/2016/11/features/while-the-church-sleeps/?search=1 [accessed: 21/12/2019]

which is the seduction of the church by culture. This is a four stage process.

1. *Assumption*: when some idea in modern life is assumed to be worthwhile and superior to Christian belief. (C.R.T.; BLACK LIVES MATTER)

2. *Abandonment*: so whatever in the Christian faith doesn't fit in with the new assumption is either modified or jettisoned.

3. *Adaptation*: something new is assumed, something old is abandoned, and everything else is adapted so that while what the church is espousing still has some semblance of genuine Christianity, it is significantly modified.

4. *Assimilation*: what is left is absorbed by the modern world and effectively taken over. What passes for Christianity is simply reflecting back to the world its own values and ideas in a thinly veiled Christian dress. Christian words are used, but the Christian content is removed. This is another instance of Marcuse's strategy to 'break the established universe of meaning'.[15]

The Tower of Babel is being built, the secularists are the architects and some church leaders (including bishops) and their advisors are the artisans. The problem which arises when the Church does this was bluntly put by Reinhold Niebuhr:

---

15 See Guinness, *Prophetic Untimeliness*, pp. 56–67.

The modern church regards this mundane interest as its social passion. But it is also the mark of its slavery to society. <u>Whenever religion feels completely at home in the world, it is the salt which has lost its savour. If it sacrifices the strategy of renouncing the world it has no strategy by which it may convict the world of sin.</u>[16]

Evangelicals as 'Useful Idiots'

Evangelicals are prone to think that they would never be tempted to go down this route. But as we have seen, the all-pervading nature of cultural Marxism and the subversive methods it employs can take evangelicals unawares as much as anyone else. Here is a pertinent observation by David Robertson of what has happened to some evangelicals in the Church of Scotland on the homosexuality debate:

Over ten years ago when the whole SSM and homosexuality debate began in the C of S [Church of Scotland] I got in enormous trouble and 'hurt' people for saying that the evangelicals were being suckered by the Establishment. The response was that this was a battle that they would win, that two evangelicals had been invited on to the panel to investigate the matter that an evangelical was going to become Moderator, etc. But they were suckered. Big time. The evangelicals were never allowed to outnumber the liberals. The only reason they were invited on to

---

16 Reinhold Niebuhr, *Does Civilization Need Religion? A Study in the Social Resources and Limitations of Religion in Modern Life* (New York: Macmillan, 1927), p. 166.

these groups was to enable them to keep their fellow evangelicals in line. They were invited to the table but they were not allowed any say in the menu. They were outmanoeuvred every time by fine words, appeals to unity (and to pride), threats and empty promises of jam tomorrow. I have to say that from a liberal perspective it was a brilliant strategy that largely worked—mainly because the evangelicals were leaderless, clueless and blinded by a myopic fixation with what they hoped the Church of Scotland could be, not what it really is—(as well as a genuine concern for their own congregations). Most evangelicals stayed in, but not to fight. Now they have been reassimilated into the Establishment to such a degree that they are completely toothless.[17]

The same is now happening to evangelicals within the Church of England.

The acute unpreparedness of Christians in the West for what is happening has been well expressed by Rod Dreher:

In my travels around the country, one thing has become crystal clear to me. Christians are not prepared for the social consequences of the profound cultural shifts—especially in more secular parts of the nation. They're afraid to say what they believe, not because they face the kind of persecution that Christians face overseas but because they're simply not prepared for

---

17 David Robertson, 'The Lion has Whimpered', https://theweeflea.com/2018/03/28/the-lion-has-whimpered/amp/?__twitter_impression=true [accessed: 21/12/2019]

any meaningful adverse consequences in their careers or
with their peers.[18]

There is, however, a third way exemplified by Paul in
1 Corinthians 9, namely, *cognitive and cultural negotiation*,
holding firm to the faith delivered once and for all to the
saints and being flexible in how this is expressed—'being
all things to all men in order to save some'. Paul's way
brings us into cultural engagement with the Gospel.

Courageous Refusal

With confidence in the reality that is in Christ (genuine
theology), the church must eschew seductive approaches
to accommodate to culture and instead embrace a more
costly path.

It was C.S. Lewis who pointed out that the strength of
the Church's apologetic lay in going against the spirit of
the age. In his essay, 'Christian Apologetics Today,' written
at the same time as *That Hideous Strength,* he outlines the
basis for what he calls 'resistance thinking.'[19] This is:

---

18 Rod Dreher, 'Building The Fortifications', https://www.theamericanconservative.
    com/dreher/resistance-countercultural-benedict-option-christian-david-french/
    [accessed: 21/12/2019]

19 Os Guinness, *Prophetic Untimeliness—A Challenge to the Idol of Relevance* (Grand
    Rapids: Baker Books, 2003), cf. C.S. Lewis, 'Christian Apologetics' in *God in
    the Dock: Essays on Theology and Ethics* ed. by Walter Hooper (Grand Rapids:
    Eerdmans, 1994), pp. 89–103. The former student of Lewis, Harry Blamires, argues
    that Christian believers have much going for them in exposing the inadequacies
    of secularist philosophy provided they don't try to play the liberal game of having
    it both ways: 'If it is the prime Christian duty to shake people from their reliance
    upon secular criteria (as we should say today) from setting their hearts on things
    beneath (as our forefathers would have put it), then we should take note that the

A way of thinking that balances the pursuit of relevance on the one hand with a tenacious awareness of those elements of the Christian message that don't fit in with any contemporary age on the other. Emphasize only the natural fit between the gospel and the spirit of the age and we will have an easy, comfortable gospel that is closer to our age than to the gospel—all answers to human aspirations, for example, and no mention of self-denial and sacrifice. But emphasize the difficult, the obscure, and even the repellent themes of the gospel, certain that they too are relevant even though we don't know how, and we will remain true to the full gospel. And, surprisingly, we will be relevant not only to our own generation but also the next, and the next and the next [...] Resistance thinking, then, is the way of relevance with faithfulness.[20]

Similarly, Harry Blamires writes:

intellectual environment is not wholly unfavourable to our case [...] Distrust of current secular criteria is prevalent over fields of thought little touched by Christian thinking. If one were to represent by diagram the relationship of two bodies of people in our Western world—firstly, Christians; secondly, people who distrust secular criteria—we should find ourselves with two rectangles only partially overlapping. The grey area of overlap alone represents healthy thinking, for it represents Christians who reject dominant secularist philosophies. Of the two 'white' areas, the one represents critics of the modern world who have no faith to give a positive meaning to their distrust and can therefore only resort to cynicism and despair. The other 'white' area represents Christians who are trying to have it both ways, to worship God and Mammon together, to serve the kingdom of God and to acquiesce in the values of a hedonistic and materialistic society.' Harry Blamires, *Where do we Stand? An Examination of the Christian's Position in the Modern World* (London: SPCK, 1980), p. 10.

20 Guinness, *Prophetic Untimeliness*, p. 20.

Christians have always accepted that their spiritual and moral position vis-à-vis the unbelieving world does not in essentials change. Our reliance upon the Bible as the Word of God presupposes that advice given in one age is valid for another. The pattern of Christian preaching established over the centuries is based on the assumption that the Christian message is unalterable in its essentials.[21]

Both the feasibility and desirability from a Biblical viewpoint of 'going against the flow' is borne out by various studies. A number of years ago Dean Kelley showed that by and large conservative churches grow and liberal churches decline because liberal churches offer commodities such as 'fellowship, entertainment and knowledge' which are also provided by secular institutions, while conservative churches offer 'the one incentive which is unique to churches': salvation, 'the promise of supernatural life after death.'[22]

Stark and Finke have drawn attention to the self-destructive nature of theological liberalism in relation to the work of Don Cupitt (whom atheist A.J. Ayers claimed to be 'one of their own'):

Why should religion without God have a future? Cupitt's prescription strikes us as rather like expecting people who continue to buy soccer tickets and gather in the stands to watch players who, for lack of a ball, just

---

21 Blamires, *Where do we Stand?*, p. 139.

22 D.M. Kelley, *Why Conservative Churches are Growing: A Study in Sociology of Religion* (New York; London: Harper & Row, 1972), p. 92.

stand around. If there are no supernatural beings, then there are no miracles, there is no salvation, prayer is pointless, the Commandments are but ancient wisdom, and death is the end. In which case, the rational person would have nothing to do with church. Or, more accurately, a rational person would have nothing to do with a church like that.[23]

In his own inimitable way, G.K. Chesterton, writing in *The Everlasting Man*, pinpointed the issue, 'A dead thing can go with the stream, but only a living thing can go against it.'[24] This doesn't mean that we should simply remain close to theological orthodoxy without being culturally engaged to cause—patently that is not the case—but it does underscore the importance of maintaining Christian distinctiveness in belief and behaviour as God's chosen people living, in the words of 1 Peter 1:1, as strangers (exiles) in the world.

The picture of Christians being in exile is suggestive of how we are to relate and witness in an increasingly hostile culture living in the shadow of the present Tower of Babel, cultural Marxism.

In *The Pastor as Public Theologian*, Vanhoozer calls one of the major New Testament themes 'joyful endurance'.[25] This was the characteristic of the early church when it stood against the world to save it, rather than go along

---

23 Rodney Stark and Roger Finke, *Acts of Faith: Explaining the Human Side of Religion*, (Berkeley: University of California Press, 2000), p. 146.

24 Chesterton, *The Everlasting Man*, p. 201.

25 Vanhoozer, *The Pastor as Public Theologian*, p. 175.

with the world and be lost with it. In Hebrews 10:32–33, the writer reminds his readers of the time they had been 'publicly exposed [*theatrizo*] to reproach and affliction'. Within the theatre of faith the truth of the reality in Christ endures. Unlike the Tower of 'hideous strength' which eventually collapses under its own weight, Christ's building is one against which, Matthew 16:18 makes clear, 'the gates of hell shall not prevail against it.'

Courageous Refutation

This brings us to the second aspect of Christian courage, courageous refutation.

To speak of courageous refusal can appear to be a kind of active passivity, like the picture of a man hunched up against the wind, he refuses to be blown sideways and his activity is simply standing firm and not moving (the passive part). But those in the past who have made the greatest impact for the cause of Truth have also been those who have engaged with the culture, exposing and refuting it and being willing to pay the price in terms of attracting the culture's reproach.

Without doubt, one of the greatest men God used in the late-eighteenth and early-nineteenth centuries to bring about a social, political and spiritual change in Great Britain was William Wilberforce. On Sunday 28 October 1787, Wilberforce wrote in his diary, 'God Almighty has set before me two great objects, the suppression of the Slave Trade and the Reformation of Manners', by which he meant the reform of the morals of Britain. His tireless efforts to abolish the slave trade are well known, for which he paid a great price in terms of his reputation (Lord Nelson said that he should have been flogged, and scandalous rumours were spread that the reason he was so keen on freeing black slaves was because he himself kept a black mistress). His second great aim, however, is less well-known, but serves as an example of a courageous refutation of the 'hideous strength' of his age.

For Wilberforce politics could only go so far. He wrote:

> I should be an example of that false shame which I have condemned in others were I not to admit boldly my firm conviction that our national difficulties must both directly and indirectly be ascribed to the decline of [Christian] religion and morality. The only solid hopes for the well-being of our country depend not so much on her fleets and armies, the wisdom of her rulers, or the spirit of her people, as on the realisation that she still contains many, who, in a degenerate age, love and obey the Gospel of Christ. My humble trust is that the prayers of these may still prevail and that, for their sake, God may still favour us.[26]

He knew that anything else would be cosmetic and short lived. What was needed was for men and women to be brought into a restored relationship with their Maker through the Lord Jesus Christ and changed by his Holy

---

26 William Wilberforce, *Real Christianity*—originally entitled, *A Practical view of the prevailing religious system of professed Christians in the Higher and Middle Classes of this country contrasted with real Christianity* (London: Hodder and Stoughton, 1989 [1797]), p. 176.

Spirit. He decided to pen an apologetic work, now under the title, *Real Christianity*. It took him nine years to write and his publisher thought that it wouldn't sell very well and so only printed 500 copies. It was published in April 1797 and by August went into five editions and sold 7,500 copies! It is a well-argued and passionate presentation of the truth of the Christian faith and the utter uselessness of man-made religion.

Unlike many of our politicians and educationalists today, as well as some of our church leaders, Wilberforce had a realistic, biblical view of human nature—a genuine understanding of the real problem and God's remedy. He saw that *all* men and women were in fact slaves. Their freedom was a delusion—they were slaves to sin and the devil (that 'hideous strength') which alone sufficiently explained the dreadful things in the world. As Jesus said in Matthew 15:18, 'what comes out of the mouth proceeds from the heart, and this defiles a person'. Wilberforce saw clearly that this could only be changed by divine intervention.

Wilberforce used both hands, the right hand of proclaiming the Gospel, and the left hand of refuting present day ideas and values, using all the means at his disposal to effect change. This took great courage.

The same outlook is required today especially by those in positions of leadership and, more specifically, evangelical leadership. Thankfully there are some, like Bishop Michael Nazir-Ali in Britain, Os Guinness, David Wells and Carl Trueman in the United States. But the silence from Anglican evangelical leaders on these issues is deafening. Whilst claiming to be the heirs of the nineteenth-century evangelicals, they do not seem to have their courage particularly when it comes to confronting the 'hideous strength' within the established church or in the wider culture. Speaking of the way a new Gnosticism has crept into the church's thinking about sexuality, Gerald Bray's assessment is cutting but accurate when speaking of Anglican evangelicals: (AND S.B.C. , PCA., etc.)

> There is no common strategy, despite many meetings that are supposedly framing one, and we suspect that when the crunch comes, many in the leadership will do what they do best—run and hide (or as they would say, "pray about it"). Spinelessness has long been the mark of the true Evangelical, and we must expect that it will be just as much in evidence this time around as it has been in the past.[27]

Preaching *up* the truth is necessary but not sufficient; there must also be a speaking *out*. This is singularly lacking amongst the Anglican evangelical leadership and a continual source of disappointment and frustration to those who are seeking to contend in both church and culture.

In her article, 'Our Children as Gay Champions', Lisa

---

27 Gerald Bray, Editorial 'Mind over Matter?' *Churchman*, 130:2 (2016), 99–104. See also, Cornel Wilde, 'The English, the evangelicals and the elites: The school for scandals', http://anglican.ink/2019/07/04/the-english-the-evangelicals-and-the-elites-the-school-for-scandals/ [accessed: 21/12/2019]

Nolland points to another approach being adopted by evangelicals and its inevitable failure:

> A popular approach of UK evangelical churches to this issue is to shun controversy while focusing on 'gospel love'. This approach is essentially free of ethical demands, and foregrounds PC [politically correct] positives while leaving the controversial bits, such as homosexuality, for later [...] Problems with this approach include firstly the privileging of Christ's death and resurrection in such a way that his life and teaching, with their explicit and implicit ethical demands, are eclipsed. Our rendition of Jesus himself must now be censored! Secondly, this approach presupposes an adherence to a traditional Christian sex ethic which is rapidly vanishing among even the devout. Those who claim to affirm this ethic keep turning the volume down (or off!). Steve Chalke has many still-closeted allies in 'solid' churches. Many more are simply no longer sure or deduce that it must be a matter of little significance. Andrew Walker notes transitional stages from orthodoxy to 'progressivism': relativising the issue becomes being uncertain about it, refusing to speak publicly about and then being indifferent to it. Next comes acceptance, agreement then requirement. Thirdly, this approach fails to factor in the new 'normal' of many evangelical youngsters marinated now in all things gay. Those with dog collars and institutional buffers are somewhat protected. They seem too busy, stressed, pre-occupied with pastoral care and internal church issues and/or lack elemental

curiosity to discover the depth of the rot, the extent of the loss. <u>Something of a 'don't-ask-don't-tell' policy could be operant, even at a subconscious level.</u> [28]

Earlier attention was drawn to parallels between Christians living in pre-war Nazi Germany and our present situation; this also holds for the easy going manner some evangelicals are adopting towards the Church of England as it blithely embraces the new norms of the secular culture. Here we have Gustav Heinemann writing in 1938:

> We have done nothing to awaken a genuine and credible readiness to give up the official church [...] How much have we declared unbearable, and yet we bear it [...] We are neither as an organisation nor as individuals prepared for anything other than that which we have had for generations [...] In the best case, we are waiting for a great and utterly unignorable signal to break away. It will not come. There will only be signals in small doses, which will not bring us to a complete break.[29]

Similarly, there will be no unignorable signal for those in the mixed denominations in which the 'hideous strength' continues to exercise its power.

---

28 Lisa Nolland, 'Our Children as Gay Champions' www.e-n.org.uk/2015/09/features/our-children-as-gay-champions/ [accessed: 21/12/2019]

29 Cited by Victoria Barnett, in *For the Soul of the People* (Oxford: Oxford University Press, 1992), p. 100.

Another parallel exists between the present and the 1930s in terms of leadership:

> Why was Churchill unwilling to ignore what was happening in Germany in the 1930s? What did he have which far more respectable opponents like Halifax lacked? The latter chose to turn a blind eye and thus tacitly collude and, after September 1939, actively appease. Churchill was willing to know, which made all the difference. People may not be losing their lives but they are losing their jobs for being non-pc.[30]

We have plenty of Halifaxes in the evangelical wing of the Church of England. Where are the Churchills who will speak out as the Archbishop of Canterbury, Justin Welby, promotes LGBT concerns?[31]

On the 4 April 1967, Martin Luther King Jr, speaking of those church ministers, who for whatever reason, refused to speak out on the Vietnam War, said there 'Is a time when silence is betrayal.' One fears that there is a similar betrayal, however unintended, by some evangelical leaders today on some of the major issues facing the church and culture which we have been expounding in this book.

---

30 Nolland, 'Our Children as Gay Champions'.

31 For example, in 2018, Justin Welby gave The Revd Elizabeth Baxter (of Holy Rood House, Thirsk) The Langton Award for Community Service, for developing the counselling, healing and inclusion of those marginalised by the Church and for theological study of feminist theology, sexual identity and of related abuse, using this to provide the Church with improved understanding and inclusive liturgies. Similarly, high-profile lesbian activist Vicky Beeching was given the Thomas Cranmer Award for Worship by the Archbishop of Canterbury in 2017.

That silence must end.

Non Nobis Domine

Kevin J. Vanhoozer in his essay, 'Sapiential Apologetics', speaks of the Christian apologist as the 'Knight of Faith.'[32] He draws attention to the Apostle Paul as exemplifying what such a knight might look like, someone who commends the faith in word and deed. A knight was skilled in wielding his weapons, both offensively and defensively as well as displaying certain virtues. One of the greatest virtues, in addition to courage (which Aristotle considered the greatest virtue), is humility. The motto of the Knights Templar was *Non nobis Domine non nobis sed Nomini Tuo da gloriam*—'Not unto us, O Lord, nor unto us, but to your Name give glory' (Psalm 115:1). It is in that spirit that the Christians must conduct themselves against the ideologies and forces of spiritual darkness which confront us today. To attempt to do it in our own strength would be to engage in the same folly as the builders of the Tower of Babel. This is *God's* battle and we are to employ God's methods of prayer, proclamation, persuasion and be willing to undergo pain in doing so. The result will be that whatever the particular outcome for Christians (such as martyrdom and estrangement), God's glory will be assured.

James Davison Hunter has argued that what ultimately makes the decisive difference in changing the world are not simply great men with great ideas, but ideas

---

32 Vanhoozer, *Pictures at a Theological Exhibition,* p. 239.

embedded in culture-producing institutions.[33] It can hardly be said that the church in Britain, including the Church of England, qualifies. Hunter contends that the church should be less concerned with seizing power by political means and instead should seek to be 'faithfully present'. He writes, 'The vocation of the church is to bear witness to and to be a faithful embodiment of the coming kingdom of God.'[34] In other words, it is to proclaim and defend the central truths in Christ as we outlined earlier and to live them out. It will not do to surrender to the non-realities of cultural Marxism or any other ideology which sets itself over and against God's kingdom (including those theologies which use kingdom language to promote its anti-kingdom agenda, i.e. those of the anti-Christ).

Since in our present cultural climate Christians will feel the pressure to keep their heads down and mouths shut, as hoped for by the cultural Marxists, gospel integrity is crucial. This is a quality of life formed by the Holy Spirit enabling each church congregation to become a lived 'plausibility structure'. We certainly need to argue and assert our theology but we also have to live it. It is not just the integrity of our message which counts but the integrity of the messengers. Postmodernists may not be too fussed about our arguments but they may find it more difficult to argue with our lives if they bear the mark of gospel authenticity. It is these gatherings (churches),

33 James Davison Hunter, *To Change the World: The Irony, Tragedy and Possibility of Christianity in the late Modern World* (Oxford: Oxford University Press, 2010).

34 Hunter, *To Change the World:*, p. 95.

gathered by God through the gospel in power by the Spirit that embody the gospel and which, in the words of John Chrysostom, 'puts to flight' the world.

On Being Against the World for the World

For such communities to be formed, communities that will stand over and against the world, for the world, three things are essential.

First, *a praying people.*

Referring to the magisterial Reformation in *Renaissance*, Os Guinness writes,

> The Reformation [...] did not come then, and in our much needed reformation today will not come, when Christian leaders sit around a board table with yellow pads and outline their vision from 'mission' to 'measurable outcomes.' Rather, it will come when men and women of God wrestle with God as Jacob wrestled with the angel—wrestling with God with their consciences, with their times and with the state of the church in their times, until out of that intense wrestling comes an experience of God that is shattering and all-decisive, and the source of what may later once again be termed a reformation.[35]

The apostle Paul concludes his great passage on spiritual warfare in Ephesians 6:10–20 with the call to prayer, of all kinds, on all occasions. One may be excused for thinking

---

35 Guinness, *Renaissance*, p. 146.

that for some evangelicals, prayer is an afterthought—an add-on to when we have concluded all the business with our conferences, collaborations and compromises. This will not do. *Non nobis* leads to prayer.

Second, a *literate leadership*.

To speak of a literate leadership is not to be taken literally! I am assuming most church leaders in the West can read and write. By literacy I am referring to the ability to read things *rightly* which involves more than being able to pronounce words on a page or understanding the meaning of a poster. It involves possessing basic information (knowledge), and knowing how to apply that information (wisdom) so we might thrive.[36]

To be sure, there is the need for biblical literacy. This is the ability to interpret particular passages in the light of the whole (*canonical literacy*), following a story or theme which recognises unity and diversity, yet recognising that the Old Testament and New Testament belong together (*biblical theology*), understanding the main truths of Scripture and how they relate (*systematic theology*) as well as reading our world in the light of the Biblical text knowing that for whatever superficial differences in culture, Christians today still stand in the same flow of redemption-history (*pastoral theology*).

THE IDEAL PASTORAL ABILITY

---

36 See for example E.D. Hirsch's definition of cultural literacy, 'To be culturally literate is to possess the basic information needed to thrive in the modern world.' *Cultural Literacy: What Every American Needs to Know* (New York: Vintage Books, 1988), p. xiii.

However, there is also the need for *cultural literacy*. Culture is, as Vanhoozer explains in *The Pastor as Public Theologian*, 'the world of meaning in which a people dwell, a world presented in various works of meaning [...] that communicate a society's beliefs and values.'[37] If pastors do not know the culture in which their people 'live, move and have their being' they will not be able to minister to them effectively. And if this doesn't happen there will be a disconnect between what is preached on Sunday and what is encountered on Monday leading to 'cognitive dissonance'. One of the maxims of war is 'know your enemy', and presumably if one is to engage effectively, one must also 'know the territory' in which the fight is to take place. Not educating Christians about what is taking place in their society, (exposing the influence of the 'hideous strength') will be like sending a soldier out with 'the sword of the Spirit' (we have 'preached the Word' after all), without instructing them how to wield it and against whom. Vanhoozer explains:

> The so-called 'culture wars' are really a symptom of a deeper problem: the fact that Christians struggle not against flesh and blood, nor against food and film, but against the powers and principalities that seek to capture our minds and hearts. Cultural literacy is the ability to 'read' or make sense of what is happening in our contemporary situation.[38]

---

37 Vanhoozer, *The Pastor as Public Theologian*, pp. 115–116.
38 Vanhoozer, *The Pastor as Public Theologian*, p. 16.

Evangelical church leaders must get up to speed on what is happening to help those to whom it is happening.

Returning to Charles Taylor's concept of the social imaginary, what all this amounts to is educating Christians concerning the social imaginaries held by many of their family and friends, and then constructing the alternative Scriptural imaginary, (which is actually reality). Church leaders who are culturally literate will be able to carry out the *negative* task of theology to critically reflect on how much the church has taken on board the prevailing social imaginaries (including cultural Marxism). Also church leaders who are biblically literate will undertake the task of *positive* theology helping their congregation members to understand and inhabit (with mind and heart) the biblical imaginary: 'the true story of what the Triune God is doing in the world.'[39] Vanhoozer writes that:

> The gospel is the theme and climax of the social imaginary and plausibility structure that constitutes the church, informs its beliefs, and rules its practices. No other social imaginary is as subversive of ethnic, religious, and class distinctions as is the Christian Gospel.[40]

The result, by God's grace, should be:

Thirdly, *a changed community*.

Vanhoozer again:

---

39 Vanhoozer, *Hearers and Doers*, p. 10.
40 Vanhoozer, *Hearers and Doers*, p. 11.

> At the end of the day [...] the Knight of faith is not a crusader, a wielding force, but a knight of the Lord's Table, <u>one who knows how to live out union and communion in Christ</u>. Knights of the Lord's Table are <u>grateful realists who joyfully affirm their faith in Christ, and are ready to put their faith to all sorts of critical tests, intellectual, existential and social.</u>[41]

<u>The people of Babel then and now live a lie, adopting beliefs and practices which are at odds with the reality as God created it</u>. The people of the Bride are meant to be people who have 'got real', who know the reality in Christ and live according to it as they gather and as they go out into the world which Christ came to redeem. This also entails supporting those brothers and sisters who are seeking to refute the lie and promote the Truth.

On a practical level, could not churches at least encourage their members to support those people and bodies seeking to do this, like <u>the Christian Institute and Christian Concern?</u> Perhaps some churches could go further and ensure part of their annual outside giving is directed towards them. This does not mean we will agree with every detail of what they say or do, but they are on the side of the angels and deserve not only our respect but active support.[42]

---

41 Vanhoozer, *Pictures at a Theological Exhibition* p. 249.

42 Lisa Nolland gives some <u>helpful down-to-earth advice for leaders and parents in relation to the cultural Marxist approach to sex and gender</u>: '1. Research what your young (especially) actually think and do. Rosaria Butterfield (Secret Thoughts [...] Unlikely Convert, p.16) observed how disconnected pastors often are: the job 'put[s] you out of reach from the very people you think that you know'. Be aware

Running Out of Options?

Earlier, we drew attention to the influential essay of Vacláv Havel, *The Power of the Powerless* and what it is like to live in what he called a 'post-totalitarian' society. The parallels with our society are self-evident. The pressure to conform and collude with the prevailing *Zeitgeist*, in our case cultural Marxism, is real. It is all too easy to become like the greengrocer in Havel's illustration, succumbing to 'keeping our heads down and mouths shut' and agreeing to 'virtue signal' when it is required of us. But there is another option which Havel explores.

He asks us to further imagine that one day the greengrocer snaps and decides *not* to put up slogans as was expected of him. More than that, he finds it within

---

of the closeted fifth columnists even in Bible-believing churches. They are either not being given what they need to maintain orthodoxy, or choose to 'move on' for other reasons—having their children 'come out' is a big one. 2. Address all issues of human sexuality, marriage and family life. Turn the volume up and promote teaching, equipping, modelling, pastoral care. Expose the fraud of the gay agenda (as above). Professor Rob Gagnon and John Nolland are brilliant on Jesus and gay issues. CORE's Dr Mike Davidson counsels people with unwanted SSA, often via Skype. Address the psychological and biological realities of sex (including gay sex) and problematic aspects of much SRE and programmes like CHIPS [Challenging Homophobia in Primary Schools]. 3. Promote the role of parents. Train mothers and fathers to meet their child's needs. Run courses. Parenting is their most important job ever! 4. Start parent/school groups to facilitate parents reclaiming their place as first educators. Discover what children are being taught, get involved as governors and so forth. 5. Make use of the excellent resources, organisations, courses and speakers available which can provide best practice on the above issues, if you cannot. 6. Establish a task force which tracks these matters and updates the church in terms of awareness and action. 7. Start praying about and discussing these issues both privately and corporately. Publicly stand with victims.' Lisa Nolland, 'Children as Gay Champions?'.

himself to express solidarity with those whom his conscience commands him to support. What is actually happening here? Havel states that the grocer is doing something highly significant and powerful. He is 'stepping out of living within the lie [...] His revolt is an attempt to live the truth'.[43] In other words, he refuses to play the game, and, in so doing, disrupts the game:

> The greengrocer has not committed a simple, individual offense, isolated in its own uniqueness, but something incomparably more serious. By breaking the rules of the game, he has disrupted the game as such. He has exposed it as a mere game. He has shattered the world of appearances, the fundamental pillar of the system. He has upset the power structure by tearing apart a lie. He has broken through the exalted facade of the system and exposed the real, base foundations of power. He has said that the emperor is naked. And because the emperor is in fact naked, something extremely dangerous has happened: by his action, the greengrocer has addressed the world. He has enabled everyone to peer behind the curtain. He has shown everyone that it is possible to live within the truth.[44]

Havel goes on to envision something even greater sprouting from this small mustard seed of non-conformity: the growth of a movement. This resulted in the 'Velvet Revolution' of 1989 and the total collapse of communism in his country:

43 Havel, *The Power of the Powerless*, p. 18.
44 Havel, *The Power of the Powerless*, p. 19.

The greengrocer may begin to do something concrete, something that goes beyond an immediately personal self-defensive reaction against manipulation, something that will manifest his newfound sense of higher responsibility. He may, for example, organize his fellow greengrocers to act together in defence of their interests. He may write letters to various institutions, drawing their attention to instances of disorder and injustice around him. He may seek out unofficial literature, copy it, and lend it to his friends.[45]

He describes these actions as 'elementary revolts against manipulation: you simply straighten your backbone and live in greater dignity as an individual.' This is 'living the truth'—an inner freedom which works itself out at a cost:

In the wider world, its most important focus is marked by a relatively high degree of inner emancipation. It sails upon the vast ocean of the manipulated life-like little boats, tossed by the waves but always bobbing back as visible messengers of living within the truth, articulating the suppressed aims of life.[46]

He does not envision some political organisation to bring this about, but each person 'living the truth' over and against 'the lie' in their own spheres of influence of life. This would then develop what the Czech Ivan Jirous described as a 'second culture' which:

Very rapidly came to be used for the whole area of

---

45 Havel, *The Power of the Powerless*, p. 45.
46 Havel, *The Power of the Powerless*, p. 46.

independent and repressed culture, that is, not only for art and its various currents but also for the humanities, the social sciences, and philosophical thought. This second culture, quite naturally, has created elementary organizational forms.[47]

Havel goes on to suggest not a complete withdrawal from society, but an engagement with it not least by setting up parallel structures in which the second culture can flourish without completely withdrawing from society. These would then point in another direction and, in so doing, establish cultural points in preparation for when the post-totalitarian society eventually disintegrates.

It doesn't take that much of a leap of the imagination to see how this translates with some ease to the situation in the West and particularly the call for Christians who are people of the Truth to live the truth (1 John 1:6). It neatly fits with what we have been exploring in this section, namely, what it means to 'be against the world in order to be for the world.' The biblical imaginary provides the emancipation spoken of by Havel whilst the Holy Spirit provides us with the courage to live as exiles and pilgrims or, to employ Havel's illustration again, 'non-conformist grocers'.

Havel's essay provides the basis for an application of an old approach to Christians living as exiles to our new situation, Rod Dreher's, the Benedict Option.[48]

---

47 Havel, *The Power of the Powerless*, p. 61.

48 'A Westernised form of 'antipolitical politics', to use the term coined by Czech political prisoner, Vacláv Havel, is the best way forward for Orthodox Christians

Dreher argues that the spiritual crisis which is engulfing the West is the worst since the end of the fifth century at the time of Pope Benedict. As we have been arguing throughout this book, much of the public sphere has been lost to Christians. In response to the current situation, Dreher suggests some kind of ark is needed to preserve Christian thought and practice. He points to the order established by Benedict after Rome was taken over by the Visigoths as a suggestive model. Following Alasdair MacIntyre that much of Western society is 'post-virtue', the need of the hour is not to prop up 'the imperium' but to develop communities which keep alive the moral life. Going further, he suggests we should embrace non-geographical exile and form a vibrant counterculture.[49]

This accords with what we have been unpacking in this chapter regarding the Church's response to our present crisis in the face of the new 'hideous strength'. Dreher is *not* advocating a complete withdrawal from society, a kind of 'head for the hills' approach. In their reviews of the Benedict Option, both Carl Trueman and Paul Helm affirm this to be the case.[50] More recently, Dreher himself has made his position unambiguously clear:

---

seeking practical and effective engagement in public life without losing integrity, and indeed, our humanity.' Rod Dreher, *The Benedict Option*, (Sentinel publications, 2017), p. 78.

49 Dreher, *The Benedict Option*, p. 18.

50 Carl Trueman, 'Eating Locusts will be (Benedict) Optional', https://www.firstthings.com/blogs/firstthoughts/2016/06/eating-locusts-will-be-benedict-optional[accessed: 21/12/2019] and Paul Helm, BO and 2K, https://paulhelmsdeep.blogspot.com/search?q=benedict+option[accessed: 21/12/2019]. Helm comments, 'He [Dreher] is concerned with the Christian family, with the education of the young, with

> People [...] have this mistaken idea that the Benedict Option is about retreating to some sort of redoubt in the mountains after the secularist takeover. Wrong, wrong, wrong. It is about small group of orthodox Christians preparing ourselves and our children right here, right now, for facing adverse consequences in our careers, in our studies, and in social settings. It is about better catechesis, certainly, but it is more about formation, which is to say, discipleship.[51]

Trueman helpfully summarises the assumptions of the Benedict Option as follows:

- Conventional politics will not save us. Nota bene: This is not the same as saying that political engagement must cease. It is simply a claim about the limited expectations we should have regarding political engagement, particularly at the national level.

- The church is not the world. As Rod merely agrees with Jesus on this point, it should not be too controversial.

- Christians must retrieve their own traditions as the fundamental sources of their identities. Again, with

---

the inter-generational support of the young and the fear of being lost or at best marginalized. Particularly he is concerned with the induction of the rising generation in the traditions and identity of the church, and of being a Christian. And to weigh these things against a manner of life that will currently and foreseeably lead to Christian compromise.'

51 Rod Dreher, Building The Fortifications, https://www.theamericanconservative.com/dreher/resistance-countercultural-benedict-option-christian-david-french/ [accessed: 21/12/2019]

the Apostle Paul on his side here, Rod is hardly breaking dangerous new ground.

- <u>Christians must prioritize the local community as their sphere of action.</u> Once more, nota bene: This is not, repeat not, the same as saying that Christians should head for the hills. <u>It is simply to say that they should be far more concerned for what is happening in their neighbourhood than on Capitol Hill,</u>

- <u>What we face is not a struggle within a culture but, strictly speaking, a clash of alternative culture</u>s. This is where the language of the end of the culture war needs to be understood correctly. <u>It is not that we are to surrender to the dominant culture. It is rather that we are to model an alternative culture</u>. <u>And we are to do so first in our local communities</u>.[52]

These points align with the arguments presented in this book. Paul Helm, however, draws attention to what he considers to be a serious flaw in the Benedict Option:

> Take for example the issue of education. Forty or sixty years ago the state system could be relied on to uphold a general moral framework, regarding behaviour, language and sexual morality. So that to seek Christian education for one's children by attaching them to a Christian school was regarded by the state system as over-protection. The simple argument was 'If sooner or later children grow up and have to take their place in the wider world, the sooner they meet such knocks as

---

52 Trueman, 'Eating Locusts will be (Benedict) Optional'.

they'll receive when they grow up the better'. The state school was regarded as a microcosm of wider society. Knocks received at school foreshadowed the wider knocks of life. We did not realize that what was then regarded as normality, permanence, was rather fragile and rose-tinted. 'Normality' was in fact the last waltz of Victorian and Edwardian social mores, kept in place by legislation. Remove that legislation (as it is now largely removed) and it lost its support in the new generations. What was change to the older was normality to the newer. One of the features of modern western societies hastening change is how they have come to identify morality with legality.[53]

This is a fair description of what has happened and why, understandably, an increasing number of Christians are deciding to home-school their children. Helm sees that one of the ultimate goals of the Benedict Option is the eventual re-christianisation of society. Helm suggests that what is missing in Dreher's alternative is a recognition of the distinctiveness of the 'two kingdoms', the Kingdom of God/Christ and the kingdom of the world:

> Christ refers to 'his kingdom' as having spiritual, ethical and political consequences, and it is defined or characterised without any positive references to the kingdoms of this world.

I am not sure that Dreher would particularly disagree, especially with Helm's conclusion,

---

53 Helm, 'BO and 2K'.

How we relate to a decaying culture and society is a matter of the individual Christian and the family. You may think that the Benedict Option is for you and your house. Others may be able to make a career in Caesar's household, or as a slave, or as tentmakers, (to give New Testament options). Let everyone be fully persuaded in his own mind.

But Helm may be overstating the importance of the individual at the expense of the church community. If Dreher is following Havel, as he claims, then there is no difficulty in emphasising the significant impact of individuals who live according to the Truth (Christ's Kingdom), who in turn belong to Gospel communities living out their faith in both the Church and the world, individually and corporately. As Havel puts it,

> The primary purpose of the outward direction of these movements is always, as we have seen, to have an impact on society, not to affect the power structure, at least not directly and immediately [...] they demonstrate that living within the truth is a human and social alternative and they struggle to expand the space available for that life [...] they shatter the world of appearances and unmask the real nature of power. They do not assume a messianic role [...] nor do they want to lead anyone. They leave it up to each individual to decide what he will or will not take from their experience and work.[54]

---

54 Havel, *The Power of the Powerless*, p. 65.

This seems very much like 'two kingdoms' language to me.

When All is Said and Done

When all is said and done there will always be *more* to be said and *more* to be done. What we are facing today is a 'hideous strength' far more fearsome and all-embracing than Lewis envisaged over 70 years ago. The technology available is far more potent and far-reaching in its ability to capture imaginations and minds than at any point in the world's history. The political will of the opponents of Christianity is strong and unrelenting. The Church by and large appears confused and compromising. The stakes are incredibly high: nothing less than the survival of a civilization and the eternal well-being of countless souls.

What are we to do?

We have already outlined some things which are necessary and these cannot be shirked. But what we must exercise is precisely the very thing that was denied at Babel, faith in God. As Os Guinness explains in *Renaissance*, 'The time has come to trust God, move out, sharing and demonstrating the good news, following his call and living out our callings in every area of our lives, and then leave the outcome to him.'[55]

Returning to Lewis's story with which we began and the episode of Genesis 11 which the story illustrates—it was not by devising some clever scheme to out-manoeuvre the

---

55 Guinness, *Renaissance*, p. 148.

plotters of N.I.C.E. that final victory was accomplished, nor was it by God searching out a few righteous men like Noah that the builders of the Tower were thrown into confusion; <u>it was ultimately by a special intervention of God. We can say that God has already intervened in the person of his Son, and that he continues, as he sees fit, to intervene by the work of his Holy Spirit as the gospel is proclaimed and lived out in all its fullness</u>. We pray that he will do so again so that it will not be to us, but to him that the glory goes.

Postscript

HAVING COMPLETED THE MAJOR PART OF THIS BOOK events have taken place on a global scale which depict a vigorous unleashing of 'that hideous strength' we have been considering.

As I write, the seismic effects of the disturbing death of George Floyd in Minneapolis in June 2020 are being acutely felt, particularly in the West. What are designated as mass protests in major cities in the USA, UK and Europe involving tens of thousands of people under the banner of 'Black Life Matters' have taken many by surprise for their magnitude and stridency. In Britain such mass gatherings are considered to be of greater virtue than that of 'saving lives' from the Covid 19 menace through social distancing and observing strict societal lockdown. The former Archbishop of York, John Sentamu, applauded these illegal gathering in a Tweet, as 'fantabulous'. The Bishop of Dover, the Revd Rose Hudson-Wilkin, who is the Church of England's first female black bishop, told BBC Breakfast racism was killing people. Accordingly in her mind they were necessary as 'sadly the world pays no attention when we do not stand up,' adding, 'Most people have responsibly weighed up the risk that they would be taking in order to stand up ... There has been a greater pandemic throughout the world that no one has seen or heard or actually stood up for in a real way ... And so people are thinking "We're dying anyway, so we're going to stand up now."'

How might we begin to understand such a response?

Any situation is usually more complex and messy than appears at first sight and we must be careful not to simplify what has been happening in a reductionist way. However, it is not that difficult to detect in the rhetoric being used concerning 'white privilege', the call, even from the Archbishop of Canterbury, for white Christians to 'repent of their racism', the pictures posted of white men and women on their knees before people of colour begging for forgiveness, that the narrative which is framing these events is largely a cultural Marxist one.

In what was to become one of the foundational works of identity politics, Ernesto Laclau and Chantal Mouffe, wrote *Hegemony and Socialist Strategy*,[1] which builds on Gramsci in order to find a way for the Left to establish its own hegemony to bring about what they term, 'radical democracy.' They argue that given the social complexity that now exists, what is required to effect social change

---

1   Ernesto Laclau and Chantal Mouffe, *Hegemony and Socialist Strategy* (London: Verso, 1985).

is not simply the mobilisation of a single class (the proletariat) but a bringing together under one umbrella all the diverse groups which are engaged in their own struggles: urban, ecological, feminist, anti-racist, ethnic, sexual minorities. They argue that the narrative which will enable the energy of these disparate groups to be harnessed for social change is the use of *power*. This is a product of the social organisation of Western society, they say, which is not only capitalist but inherently sexist, patriarchal and racist. Whilst in recent years many shrill voices have been raised highlighting the 'big three' evils of our day, it is the last one—that of inherent racism—which has taken centre stage and is the concern of many in the mass crowds on the streets of our cities accompanied by a good deal of rage.

Laclau and Mouffe propose that part of the socialist strategy to bring about the new Hegemony of the Left is for what they call external 'actors' to those who are in unequal power relations to draw attention to the fact. Thus advocates of identity politics and intersectionality incessantly remind us that our societies are racist, sexist, homophobic, transphobic, Islamophobic and the list goes on. These oppressions form part of an interlocking web which somehow must be unpicked if radical democracy is to be achieved. Such an 'unpicking' is now occurring big time on both sides of 'the pond.'

At the moment, racial oppression is the blue touch paper being lit by 'external actors' such as the Bishop of Dover, Labour MP Dawn Butler and many others (including celebrities in the USA who have paid the bail of those arrested for rioting). When it is claimed (but not empirically shown) that English or American society is 'systemically' racist and that not to explicitly support BLM is itself a racist act ('silence is violence') then the neo-Marxist meme is very much in evidence. This is not to deny that individuals or political groupings exist who are avowedly racist and need to be challenged, or that none of us have prejudices, racist or otherwise which need to be checked; but to see *everything* in terms of identity politics is hardly a formula for harmony, quite the opposite, it will harden present divisions and give rise to new ones.

The Marxist basis for BLM is clear in their website[2] with the aim 'to dismantle imperialism, capitalism, white supremacy, patriarchy and the state structures.' Elsewhere they say they want to free black people from oppression by disrupting the Western-prescribed nuclear family structure, to be accomplished by fostering a queer-affirming network, and freeing society from the tight grip of heteronormative thinking, dismantling cisgender privilege. Here is one vibrant offspring of the Frankfurt School.

There are three destructive effects of the Laclau and Mouffe strategy which is now in full flow in our Western societies.

First, *everything becomes politicised and weaponised*. In this respect Marx has won in that everything has taken

---

2   blacklivesmatter.com

on universal political significance. This is simply part of the intuitive way in which we all think about society—whether we're on the Right or the Left or somewhere in between. For example, at the 2020 Oscar award ceremony, Joaquin Phoenix presented himself as a 'voice for the voiceless.' What was striking was how unsurprisingly Woke the list of the voiceless was; 'Gender inequality, racism, queer rights, animal rights—equality ...' One might want to respectfully ask what sort of equality did Mr Phoenix have in mind, after all there would not be many of us who could afford a Stella McCartney 'tux,' even if had had been worn on more than one occasion by Mr Phoenix? Would he wish to share out his $4.5 million dollar fee for playing the 'Joker' with the other lesser actors on the set in the name of 'equality'? The point remains—*everything* is political.

The tragic case of George Floyd is a prime example of politicising and weaponising. The leap from the savage taking of the life of a black man, regardless of what he may or may not have done, by a rogue policeman, to the claim that racism is systemic in the Minneapolis police force or every police force or Western society as a whole, is a massive one to make. Why could this policeman not simply be one 'bad apple' who in due course will get his just deserts? Must this dreadful event invariably be construed as the tip of an iceberg, the unacceptable face of white racism which runs wide and deep throughout American society? The answer is 'yes', if *a priori* according to the neo-Marxist paradigm all capitalist societies are inherently racist (and you would expect nothing less from the guardians of such societies, especially if they are white and male). Surely in such cases time needs to be taken to delve a little deeper and think a little more clearly on what other explanations might exist? But if *the* issue is the revolution, allowing time for reflection is the last thing you want to encourage.

Douglas Murray makes the shrewd observation that in the presentation of 'rights' the social justice campaigners tend to make their case at its most inflammatory. He writes, 'Their desire is not to heal but to divide, not to placate but to inflame, not to dampen but to burn. In this again the last part of the Marxist substructure is glimpsed. If you cannot rule a society—or pretend to rule it, or try to rule it and collapse everything—then you can do something else. In a society that is alive to its faults, and though imperfect remains a better option than anything else on offer, you sow doubt, division, animosity and fear. Most effectively you can try to make people doubt absolutely everything. Make them doubt whether the society they live in is good at all. Make them doubt that people are really treated fairly. Make them doubt whether there are any such groupings as men and women. Make them doubt almost everything. And then present yourself as having the answers: the grand, overarching, interlocking set of answers that will bring everyone to some perfect place, the details of which will follow in the post.'[3]

Secondly, *we are doomed to perpetual conflict*. The

---

3 Douglas Murray, *The Madness of Crowds* (Bloomsbury Continuum, 2019), pp 247–248

cultural Marxist focus on groups, at the expense of the individual, coupled with the fact that equality of outcomes can never be realised, means that conflict will be endless. One of the desperate features of our society is that of grievance and vengefulness which are multiplied and amplified with breathtaking speed via the social media. The rage, what Nietzsche called *ressentiment*, displayed towards those who are 'Other is both frightening and shameful, and we are seeing this being unleashed almost without restraint in many of the BLM demonstrations across the United States and Europe. The very real danger, of course, is that there will be a terrible pushback, for how much longer will, for example, young white blue collar men, put up with being berated as the cause of inequalities simply because they are white males? If such pushback occurs, this will simply reinforce the Cultural Marxist narrative like a self-fulfilling prophecy—white men are oppressive.

Thirdly, *truth is sacrificed on the altar of ideology*. When Heather Mac Donald, the author of *The War on Cops: How the New Attack on Law and Order Makes Everyone Unsafe*, was invited to speak at Claremont McKenna College in 2017, many students objected to her being given a platform because it would be tantamount to 'condoning violence against Black people.' The students wrote, 'Historically, white supremacy has venerated the idea of objectivity, and wielded a dichotomy of "subjectivity vs. objectivity" as a means of silencing oppressed peoples. The idea that there is a single truth—"the Truth"—is a construct of the Euro-West …'[4] <u>Matters of truth are simply discarded as a case of 'Euro-West construction' in order to silence oppressed people groups.</u> This is as clear an instance of 'Bulverism'. <u>To show how fallacious the argument is, all one needs to do is to ask whether the statement that the alleged dichotomy between subjectivity and objectivity is itself an objective statement, in which case it is conceded that there *is* such a thing as objectivity and thus not the sole preserve or construction of the Euro-West. If it is subjective, it can be discarded as being of little consequence and we can all move on.</u> The important point is that <u>reasoned discourse is at a discount, thus leaving society vulnerable to the prey of those who have the loudest voices. <u>Truth is essential to freedom</u></u>.

<u>In the West we are living at a time when heresy is alive and well together with its accompanying hysteria and derangement</u>.

The high priestess of modern feminism, Germaine Greer, has been excommunicated from the 'church' of feminism—declared to be a 'non-feminist' by Eve Hodgson.

Global star Kanye West has been thrown out of the 'church' of black, denounced as being non-black by T-Nehisi Coates.

The entrepreneur, Peter Thiel, though 'married' to a man, has been evicted from the 'church' of gay by Jim Downs.

---

4   Letter of April 17th to be viewed on archive.is/Dm2DN

What is striking is the religious 'feel' of street level cultural Marxism. This is again illustrated by protests sparked by the death of George Floyd and the action of the BLM movement. The act of 'taking the knee' has a decidedly religious association. This is not a mere bow of the head, but a genuflection, a sign of reverence or obeisance of the kind required by Roman Emperors which Christians refused to do. It is considered an act of racism not to openly declare that one is anti-racist, again resembling what was required of the populace by Rome in relation to confessing fealty to Caesar. The kneeling of white people before black people confessing the sins of their race echoes the doctrine of original sin, the act of repentance in hope of atonement. The tearing down of statues allegedly associated with racism bears more than a passing resemblance to the destruction of the altars to Baal and Asherah poles (2 Kings 23), as well as the desecration of the dead, as happened with the body of John Wycliffe.

So many are willingly disappearing down the rabbit hole in order to embrace the semantic laissez-faire of Humpty Dumpty with a vengeance, such that words not only mean whatever we want them to mean, but become weapons of mass deception to denigrate those considered to be violators of the new sacred orthodoxy of identity politics: the brutal game in which winners are victims, and losers are the privileged. We all now find ourselves in the Orwellian world of Cultural Marxism.

The need for the churches to take up the challenges laid down in this book is greater than ever. Christians are to demonstrate a better way, with the conviction that God has ordered reality for human flourishing as he deems it, providing a firm basis for individual dignity, justice, morality and freedom. It also injects that dose of realism which all Utopian ideologies ignore, that the world is fallen and fractured, with humans riddled with the virus of sin—such that we are, in the words of Kant, 'warped wood'. It was to deliver us from this, to form new communities called churches and ultimately a new creation that God sent his Son into the world to die, rise again and reign from heaven, sending his life-giving Spirit. It is within the church especially that the transforming power of forgiveness and reconciliation should be displayed. We should not be daunted by the challenge, for as that one-man dissident movement, Aleksandr Solzhenitsyn, reminded us, 'One word of truth outweighs the entire world.'

Works Cited

Adler, Jerry, et al., 'Taking Offense', *Newsweek*, 24 December 1990

Admin, 'Catholic Priest Timothy Radcliffe's Submission to the C of E Inquiry into Human Sexuality', *Centre for the Study of Christianity and Sexuality*, 18 February 2014 <http://christianityandsexuality.org/?tag=pilling-report>

Adorno, T.W., *The Authoritarian Personality* (W.W. Norton & Co, 1994)

Arendt, Hannah, *Eichmann in Jerusalem: A Report on the Banality of Evil* (Penguin, 1977)

Ashenden, Gavin, 'Sinister agenda to replace families with Big Brother' <https://ashenden.org/2018/03/15/when-the-silly-becomes-the-sinister-the-latest-round-in-the-culture-wars>

Austin, James, *The Tower of Babel in Genesis: How the Tower of Babel Narrative Influences the Theology of Genesis and the Bible* (West Bow Press, 2012)

Barnett, Victoria, *For the Soul of the People* (Oxford University Press, 1992)

Bartholomew, Craig G., *The Drama of Scripture: Finding Our Place in the Biblical Story* (SPCK, 2014)

Billings, Rachel M., 'How to Survive the Apocalypse', *Reformation 21*, August 2016 <http://www.reformation21.org/articles/how-to-survive-the-apocalypse.php>

Blamires, Harry, *Where do we Stand? An Examination of the Christian's Position in the Modern World* (SPCK, 1980)

Bray, Gerald, 'Editorial: Mind over Matter?', *Churchman*, 130.2 (2016)

Breshears, Jefrey D., *The Origin of Cultural Marxism and Political Correctness*, Part 1 (The Areopagus, 2016)

——., *The Origin of Cultural Marxism and Political Correctness*, Part 2 (The Areopagus, 2016)

Brunner, Emile, *Christianity and Civilization* (James Clarke, 2009)

Cameron, Nigel M. de S., and Pamela F. Sims, *Abortion: the Crisis in Morals and Medicine* (IVP, 1986)

Carson, D.A., 'A Sketch of the Factors Determining Current Hermeneutical Debate in Cross-Cultural Contexts', *Biblical Interpretation and the Church: The Problem of Contextualization* (Wipf and Stock, 2002)

Chesterton, G.K., *The Everlasting Man* (Martino Fine Books, 2010)

Colson, Charles, *Lies That Go Unchallenged in Popular Culture* (Tyndale, 2005)

Davison Hunter, James, *To Change the World: The Irony, Tragedy and Possibility of Christianity in the Late Modern World* (Oxford University Press, 2010)

Davidson, Mike, '"Gay Conversion therapy"—Is It Harmful? Frequently Asked Questions', 22 June 2017 <*Core Issues Trust* https://www.core-issues.org/news/ what-is-conversion-therapy>

Dawkins, Richard, 'The Ultra Violet Garden', *Royal Institute Christmas Lecture No 4*, 1991

Douglas, Mary, *Leviticus as Literature* (Oxford University Press, 2001)

——., *Purity and Danger: An Analysis of the Concepts of Pollution and Taboo* (Routledge, 1984)

Dreher, Rod, 'Sex After Christianity: Gay marriage is not just a social revolution but a cosmological one', *The American Conservative*, 11 April 2013 <http://www.theamericanconservative.com/articles/ sex-after-christianity>

D'Souza, Dinesh, *What's so great about Christianity* (Regnery Publishing, 2007)

Eaton, George, 'Why Antonio Gramsci is the Marxist thinker for our times', *New Statesman*, 5 February 2018 <https://www. newstatesman.com/culture/ observations/ 2018/02/why-antonio-gramsci-marxist-thinker-our-times>

Ehrenstein, David, 'More than Friends', *Los Angeles Magazine*, May 1996

Francis, Thomas, 'Animal Instincts', *Miami New Times*, 20 August 2009 <http://www.miaminewtimes.com/news/animal-instincts-6378144#Comments>

Fuller, Andrew, *The Works of Andrew Fuller* (Banner of Truth, 2007)

Guinness, Os, 'Christian Courage and the Struggle for Civilization', *C.S. Lewis Institute Broadcast Talks*, 2.4 (2017), 1–15

——., *Dining with the Devil: The Mega Church Movement Flirts with Modernity* (Baker, 1993)

——., *Prophetic Untimeliness: A Challenge to the Idol of Relevance* (Baker Books, 2003)

——., *Renaissance: The Power of the Gospel However Dark the Times* (IVP, 2014),

——., *The Gravedigger File* (Hodder & Stoughton, 1983)

——., *Time for Truth: Living in a world of Lies, Hype and Spin* (IVP, 2000)

Haldane, J.B.S., 'Eugenics and Social Reform', *Possible Worlds* (Transaction Publishers, 2001)

Hale, Virginia, 'Parent Backlash As Cross-Dressing Men Sent Into Primary Schools To "Promote Tolerance"', *Breitbart*, 25 February 2018 <http://www.breitbart.com/london/2018/02/25/backlash-drag-queens-primary-school>

Hook, Sidney, 'Marxism', *Dictionary of the History of Ideas* (Charles Scribner, 1973)

Hooper, Walter, *C.S. Lewis: A Companion & Guide* (Harper, 1996)

Hooykaas, R.J., *Religion and the Rise of Modern Science* (Eerdmans, 1974)

James, Scott, 'Many Successful Gay Marriages Share an Open Secret', *The New York Times*, 29 January 2010 <https://www.nytimes.com/2010/01/29/us/29sfmetro.html>

Jones, Peter, 'A Response to Rod Dreher's "Sex After Christianity"', April 2014, <http://www.reformation21.org/featured/a-response-to-rod-drehers-sex-after-christianity.php>

Jones, Will, *The Conservative Woman*, 'The C of E's Same-Sex Marriage of Convenience', 3 December 2017, <https://www.conservativewoman.co.uk/will-jones-c-es-sex-marriage-convenience/?utm_source=TCW+Daily+Email&utm_campaign=b4bb06aa59-RSS_DAILY_EMAIL&utm_medium=email&utm_term=0_a63cca1cc5-b4bb06aa59-556076645>

Joustra, Robert, and Alissa Wilkinson, *How to Survive the Apocalypse: Zombies, Cylons, Faith, and Politics at the End of the World* (Eerdmans, 2016)

Kelley, D.M., *Why Conservative Churches are Growing: A Study in Sociology of Religion* (Harper & Row, 1972)

Kirk, Marshall, and Hunter Madsen, *After the Ball: How America Will Conquer It's Fear and Hatred of Gays in the 90's* (Plume Books, 1989)

Kuby, Gabriele, *The Global Sexual Revolution: The Destruction of Freedom in the Name of Freedom* (LifeSite, 2015)

Lewis, C.S., 'Bulverism', *First and Second Things* (Fount, 1985)

——., 'Christian Apologetics', *God in the Dock: Essays on Theology and Ethics* (Eerdmans, 2014)

——., *Of Other Worlds: Essays and Stories*, (Harvest Books, 2002)

——., *That Hideous Strength* (Harper Collins, 2005)

———., *The Abolition of Man* (Fount, 1978)

Lind, William S., 'Further Readings in the Frankfurt School', *Political Correctness: A Short History of an Ideology* <http://www. nationalists.org/pdf/political_ correctness_a_short_history_of_ an_ideology.pdf>

Lowman, Pete, 'Chronicles of Heaven Unshackled', <https://www. bethinking.org/your-studies/chronicles-of-heaven-unshackled/5-that-hideous-strength>

Mackay, D.M., 'Man as a mechanism', *The Open Mind: A Scientist in God's World* (IVP, 1988)

Mann, Julian, *Christians in the Community of the Dome* (Evangelical Press, 2017)

Marcuse, Herbert, *Eros and Civilization: A Philosophical Inquiry into Freud* (Beacon Press, 1974)

———., 'Repressive Tolerance', *A Critique of Pure Tolerance* (Beacon Press, 1965)

McGrath, Alister, *C.S. Lewis: A Life: Eccentric Genius, Reluctant Prophet* (Hodder & Stoughton, 2013)

Minnicino, Michael J., 'The New Dark Age: The Frankfurt School and "Political Correctness"', *Fidelio*, 1.1 (1992)

Mohler, Al, 'After the Ball—Why the Homosexual Movement Has Won', 3 June 2004 <http://www.freerepublic.com/focus/ religion/1147428/posts>

Montgomery, Kathryn C., *Target: Prime Time: Advocacy Groups and* the *Struggle over Entertainment Television* (Oxford University Press, 1989)

Naugle, David K., 'The Devils in Our World', 16 July 2016 <http://www.cslewis.com/the-devils-in-our-world>

Niebuhr, Reinhold, *Does Civilization Need Religion? A Study in the Social Resources and Limitations of Religion in Modern Life* (Wipf & Stock, 2010)

Nolland, Lisa, 'Children as Gay Champions?', *Evangelicals Now*, September 2015

——., 'While the Church Sleeps …', *Evangelicals Now*, September 2016

O'Donovan, Oliver, *Transsexualism and Christian Marriage* (Grove Booklet on Ethics, 1982)

Oliphint, K. Scott 'The Most Moved Mediator', *Themelios,* 30.1 (2004)

Ortlund, Gavin, 'Conversion in C.S. Lewis's That Hideous Strength,' *Themelios* 41.1 (2016)

Orwell, George, 'The Scientists Take Over: Review of *That Hideous Strength*', *Manchester Evening News*, 16 August 1945 <http://www.lewisiana.nl/orwell>

Sandlin, P. Andrew, 'How Modern Marxism is Libertarian', 29 August 2017 <https://docsandlin.com/2017/08/29/how-modern-marxism-is-libertarian>

Paglia, Camille , *Sex, Art and American Culture* (Vintage Books, 1992)

Piper, John, *Spectacular Sins* (Crossway, 2008)

Rieff, Philip, *The Triumph of the Therapeutic: Uses of Faith After Freud* (ISI Books, 2006)

Roberts, Matthew, 'Why Pelagianism Matters (including for the Church of England)', 18 July 2017 <https://matthewpwroberts. wordpress.com/2017/07/18/why-pelagianism-matters-including-to-the-church-of-england>

Robertson, David, 'The Lion has Whimpered', <https://theweeflea. com/2018/03/ 28/the-lion-has-whimpered/amp/?__twitter_ impression=true>

Russell, Bertrand *Marriage and Morals* (Routledge, 2009)

Sammons, Martha C., *A Far Off Country: A Guide to C.S. Lewis' Fantasy Fiction* (University Press of America, 2000)

Stark, Rodney, and Roger Finke, *Acts of Faith: Explaining the Human Side of Religion* (University of California Press, 2000)

Stenmark, Michael, *Scientism: Science, Ethics and Religion* (Ashgate, 2001)

Tan, Chik Kaw, 'Fundamental shifts in the General Synod', 20 July 2017 <https://www.gafcon.org/news/fundamental-shifts-in-the-general-synod>

Taylor, Charles, *Modern Social Imaginaries* (Duke University Press, 2004)

Tinker, Melvin, *Touchy Topics* (Evangelical Press, 2016)

Trueman, Carl, 'The Banality of Evil', *Minority Report* (Christian Focus Publications, 2008)

——., 'The Joy of Paglian Sex', *Postcards From Palookaville*, 18

September 2017 <http://www.alliancenet.org/mos/postcards-from-palookaville/the-joy-of-paglian-sex#.Wxa0oS_MwWo>

Vanhoozer, Kevin J., *From Physics to Metaphysics: Imagining the World that Scripture Imagines—An after dinner talk to the Henry Fellows and Stott Award Winners,* 18 January 2018 <http://henrycenter.tiu.edu/resource/from-physics-to-metaphysics-imagining-the-world-that-scripture-imagines>

———., *Pictures at a Theological Exhibition* (IVP, 2016)

———., 'Sapiential Apologetics', *Pictures at a Theological Exhibition* (IVP, 2016)

———., *The Pastor as Public Theologian: Reclaiming a Lost Vision* (Baker, 2015)

Walton, John H., 'Ancient Near Eastern Background Studies', *Dictionary for Theological Interpretation of the Bible* (Baker, 2005)

Ward, Keith, *The Turn of the Tide: Christianity in Britain Today* (BBC Books, 1986)

Welby, Justin, *Reimagining Britain: Foundations for Hope* (Bloomsbury Continuum, 2018)

Wells, David F., *The Courage to be Protestant: Truth-Lovers, Marketers, and Emergents in the Postmodern World* (Eerdmans, 2008)

Wilberforce, William, *Real Christianity* (Bethany House, 2006)

Williams, Rowan, '"That Hideous Strength": A Reassessment', *C.S. Lewis and His Circle: Essays and Memoirs from the Oxford C.S. Lewis Society* (Oxford University Press, 2015)